SOUTHERN ROCKY MOUNTAIN
WILDFLOWERS

A Field Guide to Wildflowers in the Southern Rocky Mountains,
including Rocky Mountain National Park

Second Edition

LEIGH ROBERTSON
REVISED BY CHRIS KASSAR

GUILFORD, CONNECTICUT
HELENA, MONTANA

FALCONGUIDES®

An imprint of Rowman & Littlefield
Falcon, FalconGuides, and Outfit Your Mind are registered trademarks of Rowman & Littlefield.

Distributed by NATIONAL BOOK NETWORK

Copyright © 2015 by Rowman & Littlefield
Front matter photos: pp. iii and iv by Chris Kassar; p. vii by Christina MacLeod
Illustrations: DD Dowden

British Library Cataloguing-in-Publication Information available

Library of Congress Cataloging-in-Publication Data

Robertson, Leigh, author.
  Southern Rocky Mountain wildflowers : a field guide to wildflowers in the Southern Rocky Mountains, including Rocky Mountain National Park / Leigh Robertson. — 2nd edition / updated by Chris Kassar.
      pages cm
    Summary: "Field guide to more than 200 wildflowers conveniently arranged for easy identification. Includes vibrant color photos and descriptions"— Provided by publisher.
  ISBN 978-0-7627-8478-3 (paperback)
  1. Wild flowers—Rocky Mountains Region—Identification. 2. Wild flowers—Rocky Mountains Region—Pictorial works. I. Kassar, Chris, author. II. Title.
  QK139.R63 2015
  582.130978—dc23
                                                                                              2014027460
  ISBN 978-1-4930-1497-2 (ebook)

∞™ The paper used in this publication meets the minimum requirements of American National Standard for Information Sciences—Permanence of Paper for Printed Library Materials, ANSI/NISO Z39.48-1992.

TO MY AMAZING PARENTS
FOR ALWAYS BELIEVING IN ME

MOM—EVEN BEFORE I COULD WALK, YOU TOOK
ME OUTSIDE EACH SPRING TO SEE THE FIRST
TINY VIOLETS AND CROCUS POPPING UP IN OUR
BACKYARD. THANK YOU FOR TEACHING ME TO PAUSE
AND NOTICE SMALL WONDERS.

DAD—I AM ETERNALLY GRATEFUL TO YOU FOR
INSTILLING IN ME A LOVE OF NATURE AND
FOR YOUR UNCONDITIONAL SUPPORT OF MY
ADVENTUROUS SPIRIT.

WRITTEN IN LOVING MEMORY OF AUNT VICKI—
YOU ADDED SPLASHES OF LIGHT, BURSTS OF
COLOR, AND ENDLESS BRIGHTNESS TO THE WORLD
IN THE SAME WAY THAT FLOWERS DO. WE MISS YOU
AND KNOW YOU ARE ALWAYS NEARBY.

CONTENTS

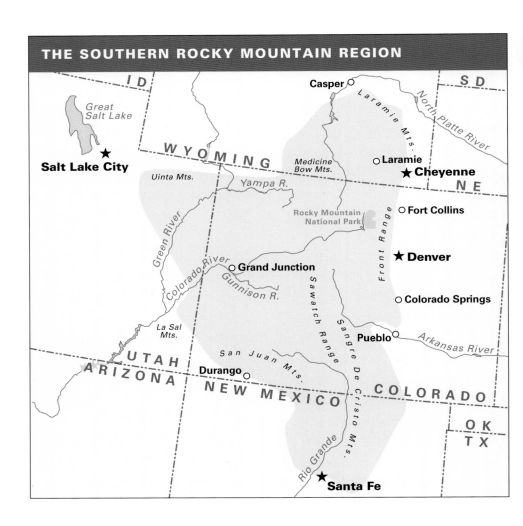

THE SOUTHERN ROCKY MOUNTAIN REGION

Great Salt Lake

★ Salt Lake City

I D

S D

Casper ○

Laramie Mts.

North Platte River

W Y O M I N G

Uinta Mts.

Medicine Bow Mts.

○ Laramie

★ Cheyenne

N E

Yampa R.

Green River

Rocky Mountain National Park

Front Range

○ Fort Collins

★ Denver

Colorado River

○ Grand Junction

Gunnison R.

Sawatch Range

Sangre De Cristo Mts.

○ Colorado Springs

La Sal Mts.

San Juan Mts.

Pueblo ○

Arkansas River

U T A H

A R I Z O N A

Durango ○

N E W   M E X I C O

C O L O R A D O

O K

T X

Rio Grande

★ Santa Fe

ACKNOWLEDGMENTS

Many thanks to all who helped me in the process of revising this book. I am especially grateful to Al Schneider, the brains behind the acclaimed website Southwest Colorado Wildflowers (www.swcoloradowildflowers.com). Few people are as knowledgeable and passionate about wildflowers and plants, and Al was extremely generous with his energy, suggestions, and photos. I so appreciate the fact that he chose to invest his precious time and share his wisdom to help make this guide better.

I would also like to express my gratitude to Dr. John Kartesz, director of the Biota of North America Program (BONAP), and Misako Nishino, data manager at BONAP, for their suggestions and help with making sure the scientific names accurately reflect the many recent changes in genetic evidence. I know they are both extremely busy, yet they managed to take the time to answer my questions and assist me whenever I asked.

For their suggestions, I would like to thank Dina Clark and Tim Hogan and the University of Colorado Museum of Natural History Herbarium, Andrew Kratz, Steve J. Popovich, Larry Friederick, Dr. William Weber, Jan and Charlie Turner, the Colorado Native Plant Society, and Larry Stritch.

I am also grateful to Katy Sykes and Rich Fedorchak of Rocky Mountain National Park, and Amy Stevens of the Rocky Mountain Conservancy for their technical review of the manuscript, recommendations, and expert advice. I appreciate the Rocky Mountain Conservancy (formerly the Rocky Mountain Nature Association) for the great work it does and its continued support of my efforts in creating and distributing this guide. Extreme gratitude to FalconGuides staff Jessica Haberman, David Legere, Lori Enik, Joe Novosad, Julie Marsh, Joanna Beyer, Kathy Brock, and Roberta Monaco.

Thanks to the National Park Service, Rocky Mountain National Park, and specifically Katy Sykes at Rocky Mountain National Park for the additional contacts, ideas, and for helping to make photographs from the park collection available. I also want to acknowledge and thank Melissa Islam, Sarada Krishnan, and Cindy Newlander at the Denver Botanic Gardens for providing photos from their collection. Thanks to Barbara Fahey of the Native Plant Master Program (via Colorado State University and Jefferson County Parks) for connecting me with such skilled Native Plant Masters and for providing me access to your informational database. Lastly, I am grateful to all of the other photographers who contributed such stunning and detailed images. Featured photographers include Al Schneider, Scott F. Smith, Russell Smith, Ann Schonlau, Steve Olson, Loraine Yeatts, Mary Dubler, Ernie Marx, Barry Breckling, Christina MacLeod, Jan and Charlie Turner, and John B. Nelson.

Most important, I would like to express my heartfelt appreciation to my guy, Nick Watson, and our superdog, Sam, for their support. They graciously gave me the time and space to write this book and accompanied me on countless hikes in search of beautiful blooms. Both Nick and Sam were extremely helpful in finding and identifying flowers, and they showed tremendous patience each time I stopped and dropped to my knees or crawled on my belly to take a photograph.

Last, I would like to express my gratitude to Mother Nature and to the flowers for making me slow down and take more notice of the infinite and intense beauty that is all around us.

INTRODUCTION

About the Region

Days lengthen. Mercury rises. Rivers swell. Winter concedes defeat and snow pours off hillsides with wild abandon. With each passing day, the sun hangs in the sky for a few minutes longer. Tiny bursts of color surge through the soil, heralding spring's return. After a long, frigid season, the hillsides, forests, and mountaintops beckon once again. You heed their call and return to the mountains, meandering through sweet-smelling pines, strolling along striking tundra, and squishing through patches of mud and persistent snow. Some old friends reward your efforts and welcome you back by slowly revealing themselves in emerging blooms of blue, pink, yellow, white, and red. Time moves on, and summer takes hold. Sporadic blossoms give way to grand wildflower displays as nature generously cloaks the Southern Rockies in a dazzling gown of colors.

Perhaps, as you explore, you wonder, what is the name of that beautiful blossom I keep seeing? Where did that name originate? How is this flower different from the one next to it? What similarities does it share? This flower guide answers those questions and several more by introducing you to a variety of the more common—and some of the less typical—wildflowers of the Southern Rocky Mountains. This user-friendly book covers a spectacular stretch of wild land, reaching from the Laramie Mountains of Wyoming south to the Sangre de Cristo Mountains of New Mexico, and from the Front Range of Colorado's Rockies west to the mountains of eastern Utah.

The Southern Rockies is an amazingly diverse region, with many delights awaiting the ardent adventurer. It includes a variety of gems: the diamond-shaped east face of Longs Peak in Rocky Mountain National Park, the dense forests of the San Juan Mountains, the snowy Medicine Bow Mountains of Wyoming, the wild Uintas of Utah, and the world-famous meadows of neck-high flowers framing Gothic Mountain near Crested Butte, Colorado.

This region boasts many of the highest mountains in the Lower 48, with 54 summits over 14,000 feet and hundreds over 13,000 feet. Glaciers have given rise to some of these mountains, while erosion, wind, water, and ice have joined forces with time to sculpt other peaks. As a result, summits vary greatly from jagged crests to rounded knobs to massive wide expanses. Tiny trickles of water begin high in the hills, flowing downward and turning into some of the continent's largest rivers, while the mountainous spine of the Continental Divide dictates which way this water flows. Substantial swaths of wild and remote lands remain relatively untouched in the Southern Rockies, allowing an array of ecosystems to thrive: alpine tundra, woodlands, shrublands, grasslands, wetlands, lakes, riparian corridors, and forests. This rich and varied landscape provides habitat for an abundance of charismatic wildlife like elk, black bear, bighorn sheep, and mountain lion as well as lesser-known critters like the Clark's nutcracker, sphinx moth, broad-tailed hummingbird, the Phoebus Parnassian butterfly, and numerous species of bees and bats. Many of these animals, big and small, depend on a diverse community of plants and flowers for their survival. Botanists estimate that there are more than 3,000 species of flowering plants in Colorado alone. Wildflowers range in size from the ground-hugging moss campion (*Silene acaulis* var. *subacaulescens*) to towering 13-foot-high annual sunflowers (*Helianthus annuus*). Numerous shapes and flower types grace hillsides, and the colors are as wide-ranging as the paints on an artist's palette.

Life Zones and Plant Communities

Such incredible diversity arises from the range in elevation, latitude, and climate that makes the Southern Rockies unique. Other factors, including variation in rock and soil type, moisture, and changes in temperature, greatly affect growing season and species distribution, thus creating regions commonly referred to as **ecosystems**, or **life zones**. An ecosystem is a recognizable community of living organisms existing together in a particular area; the plants, animals and microorganisms within a zone interact with each other and such local environmental factors as elevation, wind, temperature, precipitation, sunlight, soil type, and direction of slope.

Climate plays an important role in delineating life zones. This factor is extremely variable, susceptible to localized shifts and influenced largely by changes in altitude and latitude. For instance, temperatures typically drop as elevation increases. On average, the temperature drops 3°F for every 1,000 feet gained. As elevations rise and temperatures cool, precipitation generally increases. In addition, gaining 1,000 feet in elevation is similar to traveling 600 miles north, meaning climatic conditions and plants encountered on the highest peaks resemble those found in the Arctic. This is why, as you make your way through the various life zones, you will notice obvious shifts in plant life. Certain plants are adapted to living in cooler, windier spots, while others need shelter and warmth to survive.

Temperatures also typically change as you move from north to south. The Southern Rockies tend to be drier than the Canadian Rockies and more susceptible to enormous daily, seasonal, and yearly fluctuations. Monsoon moisture, drought, fires, and other environmental events can also add to plant variation.

On drives or hikes, you have probably observed that certain species of flowers and trees grow within a certain range of elevations. This information—the altitude at which a plant grows—is an important clue in plant identification. We will discuss four distinct life zones characterized by different temperatures and moisture conditions that give rise to unique communities of plants and animals. These noticeable belts of vegetation demonstrate the power that altitiude has to shape the environment. The primary zones covered in this book include the foothills, montane, subalpine, and alpine ecosystems.

Foothills: 5,500 feet to 8,000 feet

Grassy, flower-dotted meadows from the plains creep into the lower edges of this region, quickly giving way to the more characteristic dry, rocky sagebrush shrublands and open woodlands. At lower elevations, pinyon pine, Rocky Mountain juniper, and Gambel oak form the backbone of this ecosystem.

Foothills CHRIS KASSAR

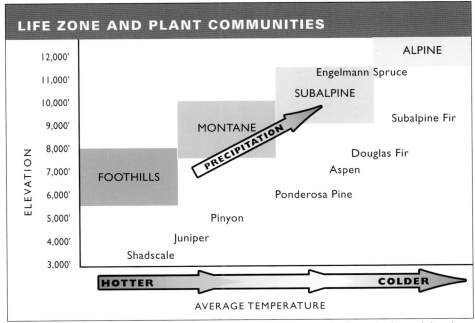

Plant communities change with elevation because elevation is a major factor in determining the climate of the life zones.

Wildlife such as western scrub jays, chipmunks, and mule deer thrive on the seeds of these trees and utilize various shrubs, including serviceberry (*Amelanchier alnifolia*), mountain mahogany, rabbitbrush (*Ericameria nauseosa* var.*graveolens*), and sagebrush for food and shelter. In the higher foothills, ponderosa pines, and Douglas fir invade from the montane ecosystem above. Depending on winter snowfall and early season rains, spring can come to the foothills as early as March, when the first delicate, lavender American pasqueflower (*Pulsatilla patens* ssp. *multifida*) pokes through the snow. Before long, other species, such as the white, starlike sand lily (*Leucocrinum montanum*) and the yellow-centered stemless Easter daisy (*Townsendia exscapa*), take the stage.

Montane: 7,500 feet to 9,500 feet

Spring comes later to these elevations than the lowlands. This region
of aspen, ponderosa pine, Douglas fir,
and Colorado columbine (*Aquilegia
coerulea*) epitomizes the splendor
of the mountains for most people.
Various shrubs like wax currant (*Ribes
cereum*) and red elderberry (*Sambucus
racemosa*) often grow in the shadows.
Mosses and lichens carpet the earth

Montane CHRIS KASSAR

and share the forest floor with flowers like single delight (*Moneses uniflora*), twinflower (*Linnaea borealis*), and heartleaf arnica (*Arnica cordifolia*). Under proper conditions, wild-flowers carpet meadows. Penstemon (*Penstemon* spp.) and lupine (*Lupinus* ssp.) paint the hillsides blue, while Colorado loco (*Oxytropis lambertii*) forms a sea of magenta. Balsam-root (*Balsamorhiza sagittata*) flowers fill valleys with yellow. Watchful hikers may spot mountain chickadees, elk, and American beaver. From central Colorado northward, great forests of lodgepole pine are common. These trees colonize areas burned by fire and pro-duce dense stands.

The montane zone contains a host of different habitats, ranging from wet to dry, open to wooded, and sunny to shady. For this reason, the montane ecosystem can support the largest variety of trees, plants, wildflowers, and wildlife, and boasts the greatest amount of biodiversity across life zones.

Subalpine: 9,000 feet to 11,500 feet

This zone extends from the upper edge of the montane forest to treeline. Dense forests of coniferous trees, largely Engelmann spruce and subalpine fir, cover the upper reaches of the Southern Rocky Mountains. They hold precious moisture and promote lush growth in this harsh environment. The narrow, pointy shape of the trees easily sheds heavy snows that would break the branches of broader species. Groves of quaking aspen dot the sub-alpine ecosystem. Streamsides and sodden ground, damp from recently melted snow, overflow with lush wildflowers. Tall, purple subalpine larkspur (*Delphinium barbeyi*) and monkshood (*Aconitum columbianum*) burst from moist meadows, while bog pyrola (*Pyrola asarifolia* ssp. *asarifolia*), Parry's lousewort (*Pedicularis parryi*), and brilliant red and yellow paintbrush (*Castilleja* spp.) grow along trails and on the forest floor. Mule deer, elk, Canada lynx, and black bear share this zone with the American marten, snowshoe hare, red-tailed hawk, and white-tailed ptarmigan.

On ridges, limber pines bend in the strong winds. Small stands of bristlecone pines, among the earth's oldest living things, may be more than 1,000 years old. At the upper limits of the subalpine ecosystem, high winds blow over the mountaintops, forming stands of stunted and twisted trees known as krummholz, a German term meaning "crooked wood." Wind-blown ice and sand prune the limbs off the

Subalpine CHRIS KASSAR

windward side of exposed trees. This weather blasting often permits growth of green branches only on the leeward side of the trunk, creating malformed evergreens called flag, or banner, trees.

Alpine: 11,500 feet and above

Stunted vegetation and the thin, rocky soil of the tundra characterize the alpine zone. On the tundra, intense cold and drying winds forbid the growth of trees, except for occasional dwarf willows. As a result, mountaintops look like foreboding fortresses of rock and snow from afar. However, for those willing to practice "belly botany," a closer examination reveals a medley of plants hugging the ground to conserve heat. These hardy specimens have adapted to extreme cold and high winds. Spring usually arrives to the tundra, or "land above the trees," in June or July. Through August, these robust plants, like the tiny cushion phlox (*Phlox pulvinata*), brilliant alpine primrose (*Primula angustifolia*), and bright old man of the mountain (*Hymenoxys grandiflora*) form lush meadows of tiny flowers with the most intense colors imaginable. Because snow can fall and frost can come any day of the year, the growing season lasts only about six weeks. This is hardly enough time for plants to grow from seed, reproduce, and make seeds. Consequently, most alpine plants are perennials, or plants that live for more than one year.

Alpine CHRIS KASSAR

While life at the top of the world can be unforgiving, a number of animals require the alpine environment for survival. Boulder fields hide peeping American pikas, small, grayish-tan, short-eared relatives of rabbits. Furry yellow-bellied marmots stand atop rocks on their hind legs and whistle warnings while others relax in the sun as preparation for their impending eight-month hibernation. Majestic Rocky Mountain bighorn sheep keep watch from ridges and cliffs, only letting down their guard to roam the hillsides in search of alpine avens (*Geum rossii* var. *turbinatum*) to eat.

Considerations

Nature varies: These ecosystems do not have perfect boundaries that fit precisely into the elevation levels just described. Although we discuss these zones by elevational boundaries, there will be variation and overlap. In New Mexico, **treeline**—the upper limit of tree growth—may reach to 12,200 feet elevation. In southern Wyoming, timberline is closer to 11,000 feet. Treeline varies from place to place; think of it as an uneven zone of transition, varying with changes in latitude or even more locally within a mountain range or state. This is due to a complex interaction between a number of factors including topography, soils, precipitation, exposure to sun, wind, snow, and ice, and perhaps most importantly, summer and winter temperatures that dictate how much growth can occur. Use our guidelines to direct your exploration, but rely heavily on your senses to identify the plant in front of you. In addition, pay attention to the fact that numerous different habitats (i.e., streamside, dry open slopes, rocky tundra, etc.) can support a certain plant within each ecosystem. Paying attention to the preferred habitat type for a species is often just as important and helpful in finding and identifying it.

Slope plays a role: Another interesting quirk of the mountains is slope. Thick evergreen forests tend to cover the cooler, shadier north-facing slopes. On the sunny, drier south-facing slopes, vegetation is typically sparser. In the foothills and montane ecosystems, grasses, shrubs, scrub oaks, and widely spaced ponderosa pines often cover south-facing slopes. The north-facing slopes bear dense forests of Douglas fir and ponderosa pine, along with blue spruce and white fir.

Plant Characteristics

Although this guide keeps technical language to a minimum, users will find it helpful to know a few special terms. Below, we discuss some easy-to-learn words that will be useful for identifying plants in any region. The glossary in the back of this book provides a complete list of definitions.

Perennial vs. Annual

Many of the plants listed in this book are **perennial**; that is, parts of the plant live anywhere from a few years to more than a century. Familiar examples of perennial plants include tulips, raspberries, and oak trees. Scientists divide perennial plants into two types: **woody plants** such as trees and shrubs, and **herbaceous** plants that die back to ground level each year, with only the underground parts overwintering. Most Southern Rocky Mountain plants are herbaceous perennials; woody plants make up only a small percentage of this high-country flora. If they are not perennials, botanists classify herbaceous plants as **annuals**, which germinate, flower, produce seeds, and die within a year, or **biennials**, which take two years to produce seeds before dying.

In perennials, parts of the previous year's growth may be visible. Perennials generally have well-developed underground parts such as bulbs or large tuberous roots, while annual plants typically have a small system of fibrous roots. Plants discussed in this book are perennial unless stated otherwise, and all plants in the book are herbaceous unless specifically listed as woody.

Leaf Structure

Leaves are important identifying features of wildflowers. To describe small differences precisely, botanists use technical terminology for the shapes, textures, surfaces, margins, parts, and attachments of leaves. It is necessary to use some of these words, but usually we describe important characteristics like leaf shape using common language such as "long and narrow" or "broadly oval."

Important leaf features to note include:

- Arrangement of the leaves on the stem: opposite each other, alternating along the stem, or whorled (several leaves from one point)?
- Shape of leaf tip: pointed or blunt?
- Shape of leaf base: tapering, rounded, heart-shaped, or clasping the stem?
- Leaf edges or margin: entire, toothed, wavy, or lobed?
- Leaf texture: thick, leathery, waxy, thin, or brittle?
- Are leaves stalked or stalkless?
- Are there basal leaves, stem leaves or both? If both, what are the differences or similarities in shape, size, stalks, and arrangement?
- Are the leaves simple or compound?

This last question about simple or compound leaves is one of the more important. **Simple leaves** have a single, leaflike blade above each bud. This blade may be lobed or unlobed, but it is clearly a single leaf. **Compound leaves** are divided into two or more distinct segments called **leaflets,** with each segment often looking like a separate leaf.

The only sure way to identify a compound leaf is to look for buds. If there are several leaflike segments above a single bud, it is a compound leaf. This can be tricky, but is important to master since several plant groups can be quickly determined by this feature. Leaflets of compound leaves can be arranged feather-like along a stalklike axis, or originate from a common point like the fingers on a hand, or even be doubly or triply compound, with each segment divided once or twice again into further series of leaflike segments. In all cases, however, the leaflets of compound leaves are arranged in the same plane.

Bracts

Bracts are leaflike structures or scales located just below a flower, a flower cluster, or its stalk; bracts cover and then enclose the flower head. Bracts are modified leaves that can be like miniature versions of the plant's leaves, or they can be very different in size and shape from the leaves. In some instances they are reduced to little pointed or rounded green scales. Bracts may be green and leaflike in texture, thin, and papery, or sometimes even colored like flower petals. The size, shape, and characteristics of a flower's bracts can be essential to identifying some species. On some plants, there are two specialized bract-like structures called **stipules** at the base of the leaf stalk. These may be large and showy, or tiny and scalelike, or they may fall off soon after the leaf emerges from the bud. In the Aster family (Asteraceae), the bracts are called **phyllaries.**

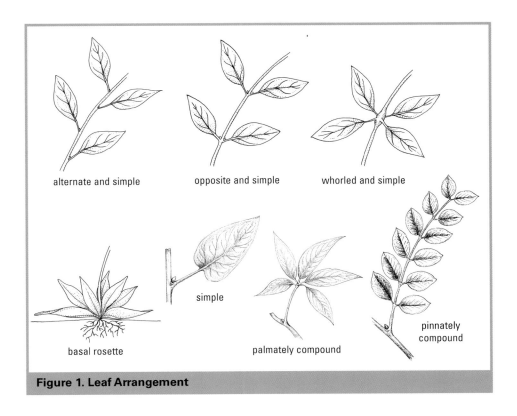

alternate and simple

opposite and simple

whorled and simple

basal rosette

simple

palmately compound

pinnately compound

Figure 1. Leaf Arrangement

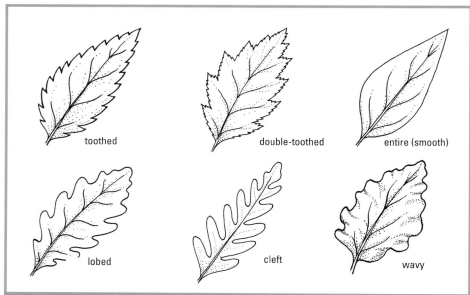

Figure 2. Leaf Margin

toothed

double-toothed

entire (smooth)

lobed

cleft

wavy

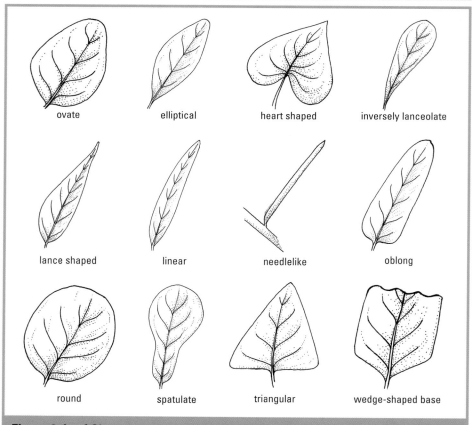

Figure 3. Leaf Shape

ovate

elliptical

heart shaped

inversely lanceolate

lance shaped

linear

needlelike

oblong

round

spatulate

triangular

wedge-shaped base

Flower Structure

Flowers are the most complicated parts of a plant. They come in an array of shapes, sizes, and color, but all flowers have one main function—to facilitate pollination of the female flower parts and development of the seeds and fruits. Flowers that are insect pollinated often have showy or fragrant parts to attract suitable pollinators. On the other hand, flowers that are wind pollinated, such as those on many trees and grasses, have very reduced flowers suited to launching and capturing wind-blown pollen without the need for showy or fragrant parts. Because they are so different and are highly modified, we do not discuss the flowers of plants like grasses and sedges in this book.

Figure 4 shows a diagram of a generalized flower. Most flowers have an outer series of flower parts, called **sepals,** surrounding the base of the flower. Sepals often are green and can be inconspicuous, but they also can be showy and colored. The sepals together form the **calyx.** The calyx may be composed of separate sepals, or the sepals may be joined or fused into a tube or cuplike calyx. If the sepals are fused, they often are represented by teeth or points around the top of the calyx.

Petals, a series of usually showy parts, sit inside the calyx of most flowers. These are what we first see when we view the average flower. The petals come in a variety of shapes, sizes, and colors, and depending on the kind of plant, there may be no petals or three, six, or more per flower. The petals may be separate from each other or partially or wholly fused together into a cuplike, tubular, or irregular shape. The petals together, whether fused or separate, form the **corolla.** Some flowers have no corolla, and in some plants, the sepals and petals are identical and are called **tepals.**

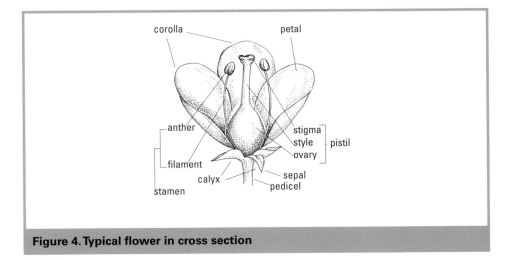

Figure 4. Typical flower in cross section

Within the flower, the **stamens** produce pollen. There may be one to more than 100 stamens per flower. Stamens typically are long, thin filaments with clublike or elongate appendages at the tip. The seed-producing part of the flower is called the **pistil**. This consists of the usually swollen **ovary** where the seeds develop, above which is a usually long, tubelike **style** with a blunt, divided, or elongate **stigma** at the tip that serves as a pollen receptor. In some flowers, the style is absent. While most flowers have both male (stamen) and female (pistil) parts, some plants have separate male and female flowers, and in some species, male and female flowers are on separate plants. The term **monoecious** ("one house") is used to describe a species where male and female flowers are on one plant, while **dioecious** ("two houses") refers to species with unisexual flowers found on separate individual plants.

Flower Types

The way flowers grow on a plant is often key in plant identification. A solitary flower may bloom at the end of a stem, or multiple flowers may bloom up the length of the stem in **leaf axils,** the angle between the leaf and the stem. Often, separate clusters of flowers bloom atop a stem. These can be elongated, flat-topped, or rounded and may be densely or loosely packed. Again, botanists use many specialized terms to describe the arrangement of flowers on a plant (see Figure 7). We usually avoid using these words except in instances where the **inflorescence** is characteristic of a certain family. For instance, the **umbel**, a cluster with multiple flower stalks radiating from a common point on the stem, helps with recognition of members of the Carrot family (Apiaceae), while members of the Mustard family (Brassicaceae) often display flowers in an elongated flower cluster called a **raceme**, in which each flower is attached by a stalk to a central stem.

Two families of flowers, both well represented in the Southern Rockies, have specialized flower structures that deserve comment. Most plants in the Bean family (Fabaceae) have a calyx surrounding five petals that are developed into a specialized form. The upper petal, called the **banner** or **standard**, is erect, spreading, and usually the largest. Below this are two protruding side petals, called **wings**, closely surrounding the **keel**, which is actually created by the fusion of the two lowest petals. A typical Pea family flower is shown in Figure 6.

Asters, goldenrods, daisies, dandelions, and other plants in the Aster family (Asteraceae) have an unusual flower arrangement. What appears at first glance to be a single flower is actually a head composed of a few to several hundred small flowers. This head

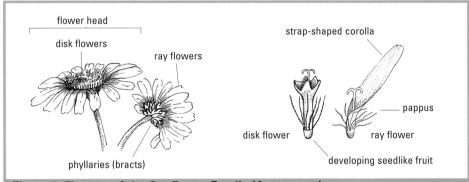

Figure 5. Flowers of the Sunflower Family (Asteraceae)

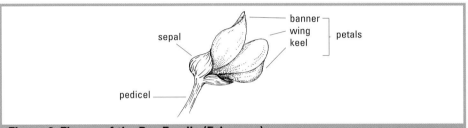

Figure 6. Flower of the Pea Family (Fabaceae)

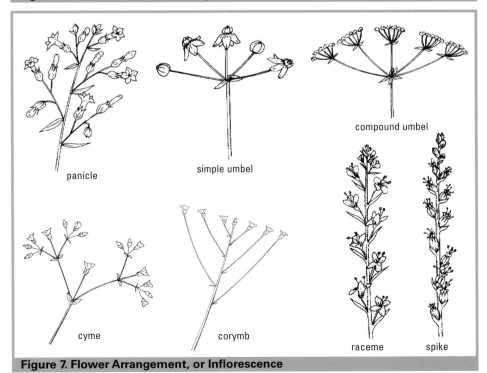

Figure 7. Flower Arrangement, or Inflorescence

of flowers usually is surrounded at the base by a series of bracts. The calyx is absent or reduced to bristles, scales, or hairs. Two kinds of flowers are produced: **disk flowers** and **ray flowers** (Figure 5), as described below. The corollas of ray flowers have a single, usually bright-colored strap that looks like the petal of a conventional flower. Disk flowers have small, tubular corollas, typically with five lobes.

Depending on the species, each flower head may be all disk flowers, all ray flowers, or a combination of the two. When both are present, there is usually a central circle or cone of disk flowers surrounded by one or more series of ray flowers, thus creating the appearance of a single typical flower, although there may be more than 100 flowers present. Figure 5 provides a diagram of a typical Aster family flower head.

HOW TO USE THIS GUIDE

Anyone with an interest in learning more about the Southern Rocky Mountains can use this guide as a tool for understanding the unique tapestry of plants found in the region. Using this book requires no specialized knowledge, just a curious nature, perceptive skills, and an eye for detail. Included here are photographs and descriptions of over 200 mountain plants. Species descriptions remain simple and minimize the use of technical jargon, with a few necessary exceptions. This spectacular region is home to hundreds of species of native flowering plants, and a book this size cannot cover each and every one. Thus, we focused on the more common and characteristic plants; however, we also included a handful of less common or less widely distributed plants that we felt filled in the gaps. We did this to ensure that this guide accurately highlights the diversity of flora found in the Southern Rockies by including a broad range of flower families and genera, habitats, and altitudes.

Finding a Plant

This book separates plants into broad groups based on flower color. Within each color, they are ordered alphabetically by family name and then by genus and species within the family. This means that members of the same family (i.e., relatives) are grouped together, allowing you to notice shared characteristics and similarities.

Flower color is a convenient means of quickly grouping plants, but it is by no means a perfect system for identification. Wildflowers, like all living things, are variable; no two individuals are exactly alike. This variation results from a combination of heredity (what were the parents like?) and environment (what are the conditions where it grows?). Just as there may be blond, black-, and red-haired people, a single species of plant may have a range of flower colors. Many plants with pink flowers, for instance, also have white-flowered forms. Some plants even have multicolored flowers. Grouping plants by color is also problematic because humans perceive color differently, making it difficult to define the variation between similar colors such as blue and purple. Different photo conditions and the printing process can also alter photo color and may at times be misleading.

In this guide, we have grouped plants according to the color that is most prevalent for the species. Once you find a flower in the field, turn to the color section that best matches the plant you see and search among those pages. If you fail to find it, try searching for variations in other color sections.

Species Descriptions

A written entry accompanies each plant photograph. The headings under each listing are as follows:

Common Name: Common names are unreliable. Most plants have several common names, and a common name used in one region may apply elsewhere to a totally unrelated plant. We have chosen the most commonly used or most appropriate common name for each species in the region. In some instances, we provide additional common names in the Comments section of each entry.

Scientific Name: Because of the confusion surrounding common names, the scientific name of the plant is necessary to label a species accurately. These names, rendered in Latin or Greek, are a more stable and universal means of referring to a particular plant; scientists across the planet usually use and accept the same scientific name. The scientific name consists of two words. The first word, the **genus**, is the name of a group of plants with similar general characteristics. The second part of the scientific name is the **specific epithet** or **species name**, which identifies the particular species of a plant and distinguishes this plant from all others in that genus. Thus, there are many species found within a single genus. In a few cases, the scientific name for a plant will have a third part, preceded by the word *variety*, abbreviated "var.," or *subspecies*, abbreviated "ssp." These plants differ slightly, but consistently, from other plants of the same species and often have distinct ranges.

Besides being consistent, scientific names show relationships by identifying species in the same genus. For example, *Mertensia ciliata*, the scientific name for mountain bluebells, identifies it as the species *ciliata* and part of the larger genus *Mertensia*. This gives you a clue that it shares DNA and characteristics with *Mertensia lanceolata* (lanceleaf chiming bells).

Although scientific names apply more universally than common names, botanists and plant taxonomists do not always agree on the best system of classification or which scientific name is appropriate. As research progresses and scientists learn more about plant DNA, they are constantly reevaluating what they know about plant genetics and relationships. If research reveals that a plant was classified incorrectly, families may shift, genera may transform, and names may change. In addition, if a botanist discovers an older name for a plant, its scientific name may revert to the oldest name on record.

Most of the scientific names used in this book reflect the name accepted by Dr. John Kartesz's *Synthesis of the Flora of North America*, which describes thousands of plants, provides over 150,000 photographs, and gives county-by-county records of every plant in North America. We chose Dr. Kartesz, who is also the director of the Biota of North America Program (BONAP; www.bonap.org), as our authority for naming in order to provide a consistent, accurate, research-based naming system that would cover the entire Southern Rockies region. His *Synthesis* provides a uniquely comprehensive source of nomenclature and taxonomy for all known native and naturalized vascular plants and serves as an international standard for multiple agencies, educational institutions, and private conservation groups.

There are many exceptional scientists studying and naming plants in the Southern Rocky Mountain region. For instance, William Weber and Ronald C. Wittmann's outstanding *Colorado Flora* is widely used by biologists and botanists to identify plants in Colorado, while others in the area rely on Stanley Welsh and colleagues' *A Utah Flora*, Arthur Cronquist and colleagues' *Intermountain Flora*, Kelly Allred and Robert Ivey's *Flora Neomexicana III*, and Richard Hartman's various works on the vascular plants of Wyoming and the Rockies. Because changes are happening so rapidly and this book is a regional guide used by readers with a wide range of experience who may be familiar with the above-mentioned works, we have included synonyms to assist in identification when appropriate.

Family Name: Plants are grouped into families according to similarities in their structure and genetics. Most scientific plant family names end with the suffix *aceae*, such as Asteraceae for the Aster family. With surprisingly little effort or experience, beginners will be able to identify several common plant families at first sight. For instance, most people are already familiar with the unmistakable flowers of the Bean family (Fabaceae), which includes peas, beans, sweet peas, lupines, and locust flowers. Being able to determine the family of an unknown plant helps a great deal in field identification.

Botany and taxonomy are constantly evolving, and family names also continue to change over the years. For this guide, we chose to follow the widely accepted Angiosperm Phylogeny Group-III (APG-III) system for naming families. According to Dr. Kartesz, "Today, unlike thirty or more years ago, much of our taxonomy is based upon high-level molecular genetics, rather than morphology. Unfortunately, many of the plant family/genus relationships that at one time were based upon morphological similarities are now shown to be artificial. This is the reason that many taxonomists have converted to the APG approach" (*sent in an e-mail to the author in July 2013*). Because of this work, several families have recently shifted; for that reason, we have put former family names in the Comments section when appropriate.

For instance, in recent years, botanists have decided to split up some plant families. Onions (*Allium* spp.) were once in the Lily family (Liliaceae), but most botanists now place them in the Onion family (Alliaceae). Ladyslippers once were in the Orchid family (Orchidaceae); some botanists have separated them into their own category, the Lady Slipper family (Cypripediaceae). The Figwort family (Scrophulariaceae) used to contain numerous genera and thousands of species, including all of the paintbrushes (*Castilleja* spp.), but based on recent DNA evidence, scientists have broken up Scrophulariaceae and moved almost all of its members into other families including Orobanchaceae (broomrape), Phrymaceae (lopseed), and Plantaginaceae (plantain).

Description: The main part of each entry contains a description of the plant. This description starts with general growth characteristics and identifying features. We describe flowers, leaves, and sometimes fruits. For various features such as plant height, leaf size, and flower dimensions, we provide an approximate size or range of typical sizes in inches or feet. Unless otherwise stated, leaf measurements are for the leafy part of the plant only and do not include the leafstalk. No size measurements are absolute, and diligent searching will reveal the odd, stunted individual or the occasional overgrown giant. However, the measurements provided here will apply to most of the plants encountered in the four life zones discussed earlier.

When identifying plants in the field, it helps to take a minute to study the plant, noting its general growth form, leaves, flowers, and any other distinguishing features. Look around for other plants of the same species. Maybe you will see better-developed or more mature individuals. A small magnifying glass or hand lens with 10X magnification helps in seeing telltale hairs and flower parts and reveals a hidden world of complexity and beauty that you would otherwise miss.

We wrote flower descriptions in this guide to help with identification, so we focus on prominent or distinctive flower characteristics. Lack of discussion of a particular feature does not mean it is lacking for that species, but only that it is not a priority characteristic for identification.

Each plant description provides the diagnostic features needed for identification, including discussion of overall appearance, leaves, and flowers. Sometimes, we mention features such as fragrant leaves or colored or milky sap. These can be determined by gently squeezing and then smelling a leaf, and by slightly tearing the tip of a leaf and noting the sap color.

Another feature often useful in plant identification is the presence of hairs on leaves, stems, or flower parts. Some plants are always hairless, some are always hairy, and individual plants within some species may range from hairless to hairy. The size, abundance, and type of hairs are often useful for identification purposes. In this guide, the discussion for each plant includes whether the plant is hairy or smooth—if this is a useful feature for identification. If we do not mention the hairiness, it means that the plant can be smooth or that the hairs are small, sparse, or easily overlooked.

The descriptions and photographs in this book are intended to be used together to identify a plant. There may be occasions when a plant does not exactly match an entry but clearly is a close relative. In many cases, this will be because the plant in question is of a different species but the same genus as the plant in the photograph. Check the Comments section because sometimes we mention similar species and the vital characteristics for accurate differentiation.

Habitat/Range: This section provides a summary of the typical Southern Rocky Mountain habitats for the plant. These habitat statements apply only to the Southern Rockies. Plants that grow at 13,000 feet in Colorado may flourish at 435-foot elevation in Alaska. Plants that grow along streams in the West may thrive in meadows in the East. This section also includes comments about the relative abundance of plants, using terms such as *common*, *occasional*, and *rare*. These are general terms to give you an idea of the relative rarity of each species and are merely range-wide guides. Species described as common throughout the Southern Rockies may be rare or absent in a particular area, and rare species may be locally abundant in some areas.

The Habitat/Range section also includes a general range describing where the plant grows. You will notice that a number of the ranges cited expand beyond the Southern Rockies (i.e., "found from Canada to New Mexico"). If the species is present in other parts of the Rocky Mountains (which include the Canadian and Northern US and Southern US Rockies), we included this broader range. We chose to do this in an effort to more broadly educate readers and provide users a larger context for where the plant grows. We thought it would be helpful for flower lovers, amateur botanists, and travelers to know what similar plants they might find in other parts of the Rockies. The ranges included in this guide are limited to the Rocky Mountains and do not reflect the entire range of a species. In this vein, we did not include details on the presence of these species in Mexico, the West Coast, the Midwest, or the eastern United States.

Comments: This provides information such as discussions of closely related species, historical uses for the plant, and other notes of interest. In some entries, we include historical or medicinal uses or mention edibility. This is meant solely for educational purposes and not as a definitive guide for plant use. Many plants, including those used medicinally or historically, are toxic and can cause harm or death. In addition, countless edible plants have poisonous counterparts that look similar. Because of the difficulties and uncertainties associated with plant identification, **do not eat, use or attempt to create medicine out of any of the plants or fruits you find.**

Final Note: Leave Only Footprints, Take Only Photographs

There is a great deal to discover within each of the ecosystems in the spectacular Southern Rockies. Here charismatic wildlife roam free, rare plants thrive, and humans have untouched space in which to wander—an unusual delight in our burgeoning world. Learning how to identify and name some of the region's wildflowers is a great place to begin discovering more. However, please remember that as an adventurer, you have a duty to leave things as you found them, or even better. Be aware of all regulations in the areas you visit and please do not pick wildflowers. It harms nature's handiwork and in some instances is illegal. Always be sure to carry a camera and a notepad. Taking photographs or keeping a journal will provide memories that long outlive even the most colorful blooms.

BLUE AND PURPLE FLOWERS

NATIONAL PARK SERVICE BY ANN SCHONLAU

This section includes flowers ranging from pale blue to deep indigo and from lavender to violet. Because purple flowers grade into pink flowers, readers looking for purple flowers should check the pink section as well.

AL SCHNEIDER, WWW.SWCOLORADOWILDFLOWERS.COM

NATIONAL PARK SERVICE

ALPINE FLEABANE

Erigeron grandiflorus
Synonym: *E. simplex*
Aster family (Asteraceae)

Description: A single flower head, 1" wide is borne on each 1–10" stalk. The 50–125 blue, purple, pink, or sometimes whitish ray flowers on each head surround a central yellow disc. The bracts have shaggy hairs that range from white to purple. The entire, primarily basal leaves are 3½" long, with smaller leaves on the stem.

Bloom Season: July to September

Habitat/Range: Common in rocky sites, meadows, alpine slopes, and near timberline tundra from Canada to New Mexico.

Comments: This flower looks much like the blackheaded daisy (*E. melanocephalus*); however, the bracts of the blackheaded daisy have dark purple to black hairs. In 1753, Linnaeus gave the genus its name from the Greek *eri* ("spring") and *geron* ("old man"), referring to either the white, puffy seed heads or the hairy species that flower in spring.

SHOWY DAISY

Erigeron speciosus
Aster family (Asteraceae)

Description: Heads are 1–2" across with 1–11 heads per stem. Numerous (70–150) blue, lavender, or light pink narrow ray flowers surround a yellow center. Branching stems bear 3-veined leaves that are openly spaced along the stem. The stem leaves are slightly shorter than the 3–6" long basal leaves. Leaves are lance shaped and only have hairs along the edges. Maroon-tinged stems grow 6–30" tall.

Bloom Season: June to August

Habitat/Range: Found in fields, sunny forests, and meadows in the foothills, montane, and subalpine ecosystems from Canada to New Mexico.

Comments: *Speciosus* is Latin for "showy" or "beautiful." Often confused with asters, erigerons usually have fewer heads per stalk and narrower, more numerous ray flowers. The bracts around the heads of erigerons are usually about the same length and aligned in 1 or 2 rows.

CHRIS KASSAR

ALPINE FORGET-ME-NOT
Eritrichium nanum var. *elongatum*
Borage family (Boraginaceae)

Description: Brilliant and tiny blue, or occasionally white, funnel-shaped flowers have 5 lobes and yellow centers. These sweet-smelling blossoms are only ¼" across. Silvery hairs cover the stems and long, lanceolate leaves of this cushion plant that grows to less than 4" tall. The leaves are thick and less than ½" long.

Bloom Season: June to August

Habitat/Range: Found in alpine environments on the tundra and open, rocky slopes from Montana to New Mexico.

Comments: *Eritrichium* comes from the Greek *erion* ("wool") and *trichos* ("hair"), referring to the characteristic hairy leaves. The similar Howard's alpine forget-me-not (*E. howardii*), found in Montana and northern Wyoming, has narrower, longer leaves covered with hairs so dense they usually hide the leaves' surfaces.

NATIONAL PARK SERVICE

MOUNTAIN BLUEBELLS
Mertensia ciliata
Borage family (Boraginaceae)

Description: Narrow, blue bell-shaped flowers dangle from tall, leafy stems. The flower buds typically are pink, opening into sky blue tubular flowers. The corolla has 5 lobes, and the length of the tube is the same as the bell-like end. Smooth, alternate leaves are blue-green, tapered at the base, and have several prominent veins. This branching plant grows 1–5' tall.

Bloom Season: May to August

Habitat/Range: Forms lush, dense stands in boggy meadows and along shaded subalpine streams. May also be found in alpine areas and at lower elevations. It is seen throughout the Rockies from Montana to New Mexico.

Comments: Also called tall chiming bells. The blue-green hue of its leaves help with identification from afar and with distinguishing it from other *Mertensia* species. Deer, elk, bear, and pikas eat this plant.

NATIONAL PARK SERVICE

LANCELEAF CHIMING BELLS
Mertensia lanceolata
Borage family (Boraginaceae)

Description: The dangling, bell-shaped blue flowers of this plant are similar to those of *M. ciliata*. The inner surface of the 5-lobed flower has a ring of short hairs. Leaves are alternate, less than 1¼" wide, and have only a single prominent vein. Short, fine hairs cover upper leaf surfaces, while the undersides of the leaves are smooth. Stems are 10–15" tall.

Bloom Season: April to July

Habitat/Range: Common in meadows of the foothills and montane ecosystems from Canada to New Mexico.

Comments: *Mertensia* flowers range from purple to blue to very light pink, depending on how long flowers have been blooming. A number of species of *Mertensia* grow throughout the region, making positive identification difficult at times. Alpine chiming bells (*M. alpina*) grows in subalpine and alpine meadows and has shorter tubes that flare into bells, resulting in flowers that are more wide than long. Leafy bluebells (*M. oblongifolia*) lacks a ring of hairs inside the blossom.

NATIONAL PARK SERVICE BY RUSSELL SMITH

SILKY PHACELIA
Phacelia sericea
Borage family (Boraginaceae)

Description: This plant's fringed look comes from the long stamens that protrude from dense coils of purple flowers arranged in a tight cylindrical cluster. The bell-shaped blossoms are ¼" long with 5 rounded lobes. The long, broadly lanceolate leaves are 1–4" long, pinnately divided into lobes and covered with dense silvery-gray hairs. Stems are 4–12" tall and are often branched at the base.

Bloom Season: May to August

Habitat/Range: This common plant grows well in disturbed soils, gravelly slopes, and open or wooded rocky areas. It is found in the montane, subalpine, and alpine ecosystems from Alaska to Colorado.

Comments: Also called purple fringe and purple pincushion. The specific name *sericea* means "silky," referring to the soft hairs on the foliage. Its cylindrical inflorescence helps with distinguishing it from other phacelias. Formerly in the Waterleaf family (Hydrophyllaceae).

NATIONAL PARK SERVICE BY RUSSELL SMITH

NATIONAL PARK SERVICE

PARRY'S HAREBELL
Campanula parryi
Bellflower family (Campanulaceae)

Description: Violet, bell-shaped flowers stand erect on the slender stalks of this plant. The ½" long blossoms have 5 pointed lobes, 5 stamens, a 3-lobed stigma, and lobes that take up about half the height of the entire flower bell. There usually is only 1 flower on each stalk. Lower stem leaves are narrow, fringed with white hairs, entire, and 1–2" long. Stems are 4–12" tall.

Bloom Season: June to September

Habitat/Range: Found in aspen groves and moist meadows in the montane to subalpine ecosystems from Montana to New Mexico.

Comments: The blue flowers of alpine harebell (*C. uniflora*) are borne on stalks under 4" tall. Its leaves lack obvious hairs. This and a number of other plants are named in honor of Charles Parry, a 19th-century botanist who spent 40 summers collecting plants in the western United States.

MOUNTAIN HAREBELL
Campanula rotundifolia
Bellflower family (Campanulaceae)

Description: Delicate, nodding lavender-blue flowers hang daintily from slender stalks. Blossoms are ½–¾" long with similar width and have lobes that take up about one-third of the flower bell. Basal leaves are round and toothed. The alternate, linear to narrowly lance-shaped stem leaves are 1–3" long. Several blossoms dangle from each 4–31" stem.

Bloom Season: June to September

Habitat/Range: Common in both dry and moist sites from the foothills to subalpine environs. Its wide range extends from Canada to New Mexico.

Comments: Also called bluebell of Scotland. This circumboreal plant also is found in Eurasia. *Campanula* means "small bell," and *rotundifolia* refers to the leaf shape. The Navajo rubbed harebell on their bodies for protection from injury while hunting and for protection from witches.

LORAINE YEATTS

SPIDERWORT
Tradescantia occidentalis
Spiderwort family (Commelinaceae)

Description: Loose clusters of deep blue, purple, or rose-colored flowers grow on smooth, weedy-looking stems with several joints. The blossoms, which commonly grow to over 1" across, have 3 petals and 6 hairy purple stamens that support bright yellow anthers. Green sepals and flower stalks usually bear sticky hairs. Below the stalks are 2–3 leafy bracts. Leaves, which are long, narrow, alternate, and grasslike, form a sheath around the stem. This plant grows 6–24" tall.

Bloom Season: April to August

Habitat/Range: Grows in sandy and rocky soils, forest and grassland openings, fields, on gravelly hillsides, and along trails in the foothills ecosystem from Montana to New Mexico.

Comments: Native Americans used spiderwort as a cooked vegetable. Linnaeus named this genus for John Tradescant, known as the founder of British gardening. A similar species, western dayflower (*Commelina dianthifolia*), grows from central Colorado to Mexico and has blue flowers above a folded bract with a long, pointy tip.

CHRIS KASSAR

SILVERY LUPINE
Lupinus argenteus
Bean family (Fabaceae)

Description: Tall, showy clusters of blue/purple, pealike flowers make this plant eye catching. Long racemes consist of numerous 5-part flowers that are ½" long, 2-lipped, and may be partially white. The alternate, palmately compound leaves have 5–9 leaflets. The leaves and stems are covered with gray hairs. It is highly variable, growing 10–40" tall. The bean-like seedpods are hairy and up to 1" long.

Bloom Season: May to September

Habitat/Range: Common in meadows and forest edges of the foothills, montane, and subalpine ecosystems from Canada to New Mexico.

Comments: Also called mountain lupine. The name *lupine* (Latin for "of wolves") came about due to the mistaken belief that lupine rob the soil of nutrients. *Argenteus* means "silvery" and refers to the hairs. Hybridization makes exact species identification of lupine difficult at times, but *L. argenteus* ssp. *ingratus*, a white-flowered subspecies common in the eastern foothills of Colorado's Front Range, stands out.

LORAINE YEATTS

CHRIS KASSAR

PLEATED GENTIAN
Gentiana affinis
Synonym: *Pneumonanthe affinis*
Gentian family (Gentianaceae)

Description: These blue to indigo tubular flowers are similar to the Parry gentian (*G. parryi*) but lack the green bands. The 5-lobed blossoms are pleated and ¾–1⅛" long. Leaves are oblong, entire and opposite. There are several flowers on the strong maroon stems, which grow to 15" in height and curve at the base.

Bloom Season: July to September

Habitat/Range: Grows in meadows, on hillsides, and in moist areas in the foothills, montane, and subalpine ecosystems from Canada to New Mexico.

Comments: Also called prairie gentian or bottle gentian. The roots of several species of gentians were used as a stomach tonic by Native Americans and early settlers.

PARRY GENTIAN
Gentiana parryi
Synonym: *Pneumonanthe parryi*
Gentian family (Gentianaceae)

Description: These goblet-like flowers have a true blue color with green bands and spotted interior surrounding the pistil and stamens. There are pleats between the 5 lobes of 1½" long blossoms. The smooth, oval leaves are opposite and entire. The stems may have 1 to several flowers and can range from a few inches tall on the tundra to 18" tall in subalpine meadows.

Bloom Season: July to September

Habitat/Range: Graces alpine tundra and meadows of the subalpine ecosystem from Wyoming to New Mexico.

Comments: Also called mountain, blue, or bottle gentian. These and several other gentian flowers close up in cloudy or rainy weather. The alpine moss gentian (*G.prostrata*) has light blue or purple flowers that are less than 1" long.

NATIONAL PARK SERVICE

NATIONAL PARK SERVICE

FRINGED GENTIAN
Gentianopsis thermalis
Gentian family (Gentianaceae)

Description: As the name suggests, the 4 lobes of this bright blue to purple flower are fringed. A single tubular blossom rests upon each slender stalk. The 1–2" long flowers have 4 pointed sepals and a 2-parted stigma. This annual plant has opposite leaves and grows to 16" tall.

Bloom Season: July to September

Habitat/Range: Found in moist areas of the montane, subalpine, and alpine ecosystems from Canada to New Mexico.

Comments: This plant was given its species name, *thermalis*, because it grows near Yellowstone National Park's hot springs. It may be confused with the lighter-colored, sweet-smelling flowers of fragrant gentian (*G. barbellata*), but a closer look will show that *G. barbellata* has different fringing, very short flower stems, and petals that are broadest at the bottom, whereas *G. thermalis* has long flower stems and petals that are broadest at the tip. *G. barbellata* is also usually much shorter and grows in drier sites.

STAR GENTIAN
Swertia perennis
Gentian family (Gentianaceae)

Description: These clustered, star-shaped, pale bluish-purple flowers have greenish or white spots. Each of the 4 or 5 lobes have small nectar glands that appear as depressions with scales and hairs at the base. The stamens protrude from the ¾" wide flowers. The long, lanceolate basal leaves taper to a slender stalk and are up to 8" long. The opposite stem leaves are much smaller. These perennial plants grow from rhizomes to heights of 20".

Bloom Season: July to September

Habitat/Range: Found in open, wet areas of the montane, subalpine, and alpine ecosystems from Alaska to New Mexico.

Comments: Also called felwort (from *fel*, "rock," and *wort*, "plant"). The genus honors Emanuel Sweert, a 16th-century Dutch botanist who composed a catalog of plants, and *perennis* is Latin for "through the year, perennial." This plant is circumboreal and was first collected in Bavaria.

NATIONAL PARK SERVICE BY RUSSELL SMITH

MARY DUBLER

WILD IRIS
Iris missouriensis
Iris family (Iridaceace)

Description: This bluish-purple flower looks much like its garden relatives. Flowers are 3–4" wide with 3 yellow-streaked sepals that curve downward and 3 petals that stick up. Three erect petal-like style branches hide the stamens. From 1–3 flowers sit atop a leafless stalk surrounded by clumps of mainly basal, swordlike leaves that are 8–20" long, smooth, entire, and have parallel veins. This plant can grow 8–20". The fruit is a 3-parted capsule.

Bloom Season: May to July

Habitat/Range: Found in wet meadows and along streambanks in the foothills, montane, and subalpine ecosystems from Canada to New Mexico.

Comments: Also called western blue flag. Roots are poisonous. Several western American Indian nations soaked the roots in animal bile and used the mixture on arrows as poison. Orrisroot, a fixative used in potpourris and perfumes, comes from irises. Iris was the Greek goddess of the rainbow, and *missouriensis* refers to the river; in 1834 Thomas Nuttall named the species from a specimen collected by his friend Nathaniel Wyeth near the source of the Missouri.

BLUE-EYED GRASS
Sisyrinchium montanum
Iris family (Iridaceace)

Description: Despite its name and the shape of its leaves, this plant is not a grass. The blue, starlike flowers are less than ¾" across and typically have a yellow center. The 3 petals and 3 sepals look exactly alike. The slender stems are 5–20" tall. The fruits are small round berries.

Bloom Season: May to July

Habitat/Range: Common in moist to moderately dry, open sites and grassy areas of the foothills, montane, and subalpine ecosystems. Found from Canada to New Mexico.

Comments: *Sisyrinchium* is an ancient Greek name for an iris-like plant. Natives used the entire plant to make a tea that cured stomachaches.

CHRIS KASSAR

CHRIS KASSAR

BRITTON SKULLCAP
Scutellaria brittonii
Mint family (Lamiaceae)

Description: Deep blue to purple ¾–1" flowers have upper and lower lips. Distinctive features include an upper lip with velvety crest, a larger lower lip with white ribs, and a ridge on top of the blossom that helps distinguish skullcaps from other mints. The leaves are entire, and the foliage may be smooth or covered with sticky hairs. Two paired blossoms attach halfway up the 4–12" square stem where the narrow, opposite leaves attach.

Bloom Season: May to July

Habitat/Range: Grows on dry open hillsides, woods, and grassy areas in the foothills and montane ecosystems from Wyoming to New Mexico.

Comments: Between the 18th and the early 20th centuries, skullcap was made into a medicine believed to alleviate tremors and convulsions; one species was used to treat rabies.

BLUE FLAX
Linum lewisii var. *lewisii*
Synonym: *Adenolinum lewisii*
Flax family (Linaceae)

Description: Delicate flowers ranging from pale blue to lavender to dark blue/purple rest on slender stalks that sway in mountain breezes. The 5 petals open in the morning and may fall off the same afternoon. The center of the blossom is yellow and ¾–1½" wide, with 5 stamens and a 5-parted stigma. Narrow, alternate leaves are ½–1¼" long. The tough stems may be up to 36" tall. The round seedpods are the size of a small pea.

Bloom Season: May to August

Habitat/Range: Found in woodlands, openings, and meadows from foothills to subalpine ecosystems from Alaska to Mexico.

Comments: Explorer and scientist Meriwether Lewis collected the first specimen of this plant in 1806 on his famed exploration of the Louisiana Purchase. *Linum* means "linen" and refers to the fact that this species belongs to the family that gives us linen.

SCOTT F. SMITH

NATIONAL PARK SERVICE

DWARF LOUSEWORT
Pedicularis centranthera
Broomrape family (Orobanchaceae)

Description: The closely crowded flowers of dwarf lousewort are on stems that are shorter than the surrounding leaves. The petals are nearly white at the base, becoming pale orchid to purple near the helmet-shaped tip. The leaves have many pinnately arranged segments, curled and crinkly, with white-tipped teeth. This small, low-growing herb reaches no more than 6" tall.

Bloom Season: March to July

Habitat/Range: Found in pinyon-juniper and ponderosa pine woodlands of the foothills and montane ecosystems of Colorado, Utah, and New Mexico.

Comments: *Pedicularis* is Latin for "louse"; at one time people believed this plant either gave lice to or cured lice in cattle and people. *Centranthera* comes from the Greek word *centrum* meaning "sharp point," referring to the pointed and spurred anthers. Shoshoni Indians made a decoction of the root to soothe children's stomachaches. Formerly in the Figwort family (Scrophulariaceae).

MOUNTAIN BEARDTONGUE
Penstemon glaber
Plantain family (Plantaginaceae)

Description: Bright blue, pale blue to pinkish flowers are tightly clustered on one side of the stem. The blossoms have a 2-lobed upper lip and 3-lobed lower lip. Flowers are ¾–1¼" long. The 5th, sterile stamen is smooth or hairy only on the tip. The opposite, glossy leaves are green or sometimes bluish. The stems are stout, erect, and may be up to 3' tall and grouped in clumps.

Bloom Season: June to August

Habitat/Range: Common along roadsides and slopes in the foothills, montane, and subalpine ecosystems from Wyoming to New Mexico.

Comments: Also called Pikes Peak penstemon. This species was first collected on Pikes Peak in 1820 by Edwin James, the first documented white man to climb the peak. The name "beardtongue" refers to the sterile stamen's hairy tip. Formerly in the Figwort family (Scrophulariaceae).

STEVE OLSON

NATIONAL PARK SERVICE

ROCKY MOUNTAIN PENSTEMON

Penstemon strictus
Plantain family (Plantaginaceae)

Description: Very showy tubular blossoms ranging from deep purple to lavender have 2 upper lips and 3 lower lips with deeply cut lobes. Numerous flowers decorate one to a few stems arising from a single crown. Flowers mainly sit on 1 side of a stem that has paired, entire, and narrowly oblanceolate leaves. This plant grows 1-3' tall and is often found in stunning clusters.

Bloom Season: May to August

Habitat/Range: Found in meadows and openings in foothills, montane, and subalpine environments from Wyoming to New Mexico. Often found amid sagebrush associated with pinyon-juniper, scrub oak, and openings of ponderosa pine and aspen spruce forest.

Comments: Deer, antelope, and birds forage on penstemons. In Latin, *strictus* means "straight" and may refer to the leaves or the erect stems, which actually often lean to one side or the other. Formerly in the Figwort family (Scrophulariaceae).

ONESIDED PENSTEMON

Penstemon unilateralis
Synonym: *P. virgatus* ssp. *asa-grayi*
Plantain family (Plantaginaceae)

Description: As the name implies, these flowers grow clustered on one side of the stem. The outside of each blossom is blue, and the inside is pinkish. The tubular flowers are ¾–1" long, and they flare out abruptly from the base. The 5th, sterile stamen is smooth and has no, or few, hairs. The opposite, lance-shaped leaves lack the heavy white coating common to some penstemons. The stout stem may be up to 30" tall.

Bloom Season: June to August

Habitat/Range: Commonly found in large clumps on hills and mesas in the foothills and montane ecosystems from Wyoming to New Mexico.

Comments: Also called tall penstemon, this beautiful flower was recognized by pollination ecologists for its value to native bees because it attracts large numbers of them. This plant is similar to bearded sidebells penstemon (*P. secundiflorus*), which has a hairy, sterile stamen and light to dark purple flowers. Formerly in the Figwort family (Scrophulariaceae).

DENVER BOTANIC GARDENS

LOW PENSTEMON
Penstemon virens
Plantain family (Plantaginaceae)

Description: These dainty, royal blue to violet tubular flowers have 2 lobes on top and 3 below. The lower lip reaches longer than the upper, and the upper lip has 2 recurved lobes. The ½–¾" long blossoms usually have sticky hairs on the outside and maroon to purple nectar guides within. One of the 5 stamens is sterile and hairy. The shiny, lance-shaped leaves are opposite, with upper leaves clasping the stem. Flowers are in clusters atop erect, variably hairy 4–14" stems that often grow in clumps.

Bloom Season: May to July

Habitat/Range: Masses of these blue flowers color dry, rocky hillsides from the foothills through the subalpine ecosystems in Wyoming and Colorado.

Comments: Also called blue mist or greenleaf penstemon. *Penstemon* means "5 stamens," and one usually extends out of the flower. Because of this protruding tonguelike stamen, penstemons are often called beardtongues. Formerly in the Figwort family (Scrophulariaceae).

NATIONAL PARK SERVICE BY ANN SCHONLAU

NATIONAL PARK SERVICE

WHIPPLE'S PENSTEMON

Penstemon whippleanus
Plantain family (Plantaginaceae)

Description: Nodding clusters of deep wine-purple to dark purple 2-lipped flowers grow in clusters atop a leafy stem. Sticky hairs cover the outside surfaces of the ¾–1½" long blossoms. The 3-lobed bottom lip is longer than the 2-lobed upper lip. A tuft of hairs decorates the tip of the 5th, sterile stamen. Smooth, opposite, pointed leaves are ½–6" long. The stalked lower leaves are oval shaped, while the upper leaves have no stalk. The dark green leaves usually are entire, but sometimes have teeth. Plants grow from 4–28" in height.

Bloom Season: June to September

Habitat/Range: Grows on gravelly slopes, tundra, and in meadows and open woods in the montane, subalpine, and alpine ecosystems from Montana to New Mexico.

Comments: Also called dusky penstemon, dark penstemon, or dark beardtongue. White variations are not common but have been found in certain spots. Formerly in the Figwort family (Scrophulariaceae).

CUSHION PHLOX

Phlox pulvinata
Synonym: *P. sibirica* ssp. *pulvinata*
Phlox family (Polemoniaceae)

Description: Five light purple, blue, pink, or white petals unite to form a funnel-shaped tube at the base of these flowers. The blossoms, about ¼–½" long, are borne singly at the top of a short stem. The crowded, entire leaves are less than ⅜" long. The sticky, hairy foliage forms tight, cushion-like mats.

Bloom Season: June to August

Habitat/Range: Grows in rocky alpine meadows and dry open or wooded slopes in foothills, montane, and subalpine zones from Montana to New Mexico.

Comments: Also called alpine phlox. *Pulvinata* comes from the Latin *pulvinar*, meaning "a cushion." Many-flowered phlox (*P. multiflora*) has longer, smooth leaves and longer flowers. Tufted phlox (*P. caespitosa*) has woody stems.

AL SCHNEIDER, WWW.SWCOLORADOWILDFLOWERS.COM

NATIONAL PARK SERVICE

TOWERING JACOB'S LADDER

Polemonium foliosissimum var. *foliosissimum*
Phlox family (Polemoniaceae)

Description: Flat-topped clusters of showy funnel-shaped, blue-purple blossoms make it easy to notice this flower. Flowers divide into 5 segments and have long yellow/orange-tipped stamens. Branched or unbranched stems grow tall; usually 2–3'; pinnately compound leaves resemble ladders.

Bloom Season: June to August

Habitat/Range: Found in montane and subalpine meadows and hillsides from Nevada to New Mexico.

Comments: *Foliosissimum* is Greek for "very leafy."

SUBALPINE JACOB'S LADDER

Polemonium pulcherrimum ssp. *delicatum*
Synonym: *P. delicatum*
Phlox family (Polemoniaceae)

Description: The 5 pointed lobes of this polemonium are longer than the flower tube. Colors range from violet to pale blue, with occasional clusters of white or pink blossoms. The flowers are ¼–½" long and grow in small clusters. Five long stamens surround a 3-parted stigma. The basal, pinnately compound leaves resemble tiny ladders. The sprawling stems are under 10" tall and woolly.

Bloom Season: May to August

Habitat/Range: Often found in the moist shady forest areas in the subalpine ecosystem, but also grows at timberline and on the alpine tundra from Wyoming to New Mexico.

Comments: Like numerous other polemoniums, this flower has a strong, skunky smell.

35

NATIONAL PARK SERVICE

MARY DUBLER

SKY PILOT
Polemonium viscosum
Phlox family (Polemoniaceae)

Description: This plant features bright blue-violet, skunky-smelling flowers ½–¾" long with 5 rounded lobes. The 5 stamens, tipped with orange pollen, are hard to miss. Funnel-shaped blossoms are clustered at the top of a hairy, sticky stem. Hairy sepals are almost as long as the fused flower tube. The leaves are pinnately divided, up to 6" long, and chiefly basal. This plant usually grows from 3–16" tall.

Bloom Season: May to August

Habitat/Range: Often abundant on rocky alpine slopes, tundra, and disturbed ground from Canada to New Mexico.

Comments: Also called skunkweed, this plant's odor may vary, depending on the race or population of flowers. The common name sky pilot comes from its preference for high elevations. *P. confertum*, found in Colorado and rare but present in New Mexico, is very similar, and the two appear to hybridize often.

MONKSHOOD
Aconitum columbianum
Buttercup family (Ranunculaceae)

Description: The showy parts of this deep purplish-blue flower are actually sepals. The upper sepal forms a hood that covers most of the other flower parts. Two broadly oval side sepals make up the body, and 2 narrow lower sepals form feet. The ⅝–1¼" long flowers are borne on stalks along the stem, which may be up to 5' tall. The leaves are alternate, 2–7" across, and have deeply palmately divided, toothed lobes.

Bloom Season: June to August

Habitat/Range: Found along streams, open woods, and wet meadows primarily in the montane and subalpine ecosystems from Canada to New Mexico.

Comments: Similar in appearance to larkspurs, monkshood lacks the spurred sepal. The generic name *Aconitum* may be loosely translated as "unconquerable poison." All parts of this plant are poisonous. Variants with white or greenish white sepals occasionally occur. Some botanists place this species in the Hellebore family (Helleboraceae).

NATIONAL PARK SERVICE BY ANN SCHONLAU

NATIONAL PARK SERVICE

COLORADO COLUMBINE
Aquilegia coerulea
Buttercup family (Ranunculaceae)

Description: Colorado's state flower has 5 blue to lavender sepals and 5 funnel-shaped white petals with narrow blue spurs. The blossoms are 2–3" across with numerous yellow stamens protruding from the center of the flower. The compound leaves have deep, rounded lobes. Stems may be 8–24" tall.

Bloom Season: June to August

Habitat/Range: Found in moist soils, aspen groves, and rocky meadows of the foothills, montane, subalpine, and alpine ecosystems from Montana to New Mexico.

Comments: Also called blue columbine, since *coerule* is Latin for "blue." In Latin, *columbinus* means "dove," referring to the flower's resemblance to a group of doves from the side or back. Other varieties, including a white-flowered form and one that is blue and spurless, occasionally grow in the Southern Rockies. Some botanists place this species in the Hellebore family (Helleboraceae).

ALPINE COLUMBINE
Aquilegia saximontana
Buttercup family (Ranunculaceae)

Description: These nodding flowers look much like those of their larger cousin, *A. coerula* (Colorado columbine). The blossoms are less than 1" across with short and uniquely hooked spurs. Leaves are primarily basal and have 3 leaflets with rounded lobes. Stems usually are less than 4" tall.

Bloom Season: July to August

Habitat/Range: This rare plant may be found hiding under the edges of boulders or on rocky slopes in the subalpine and alpine ecosystems. It is found only in Colorado.

Comments: Also called Rocky Mountain blue columbine and dwarf columbine, this narrow endemic is of conservation concern. A similar species, Jones's columbine (*A. jonesii*), has all-blue flowers and can be found from Canada to Wyoming.

CHRIS KASSAR

NATIONAL PARK SERVICE

SUGAR BOWLS
Clematis hirsutissima var. *hirsutissima*
Synonym: *Coriflora hirsutissima*
Buttercup family (Ranunculaceae)

Description: One purplish to dull reddish flower hangs like an inverted jug from a single slim stem. Four leathery, hairy, petal-like sepals with outwardly flaring ends merge at the base to create this unmatched 1" long blossom. Gray, hairy, opposite compound leaves are divided into many narrow segments along the stem. This plant grows 8–24" tall. Fruits are silvery, shaggy plumes.

Bloom Season: April to July

Habitat/Range: Found in grasslands, open forests, and dry slopes in foothills, montane, and subalpine environments from Canada to New Mexico.

Comments: Also known as leatherflower, vase flower, and lion's beard in reference to the appearance of the fruit. *Hirsutissima* means "hairy," referring to the hairs covering the flower and its stalk. Unlike most clematis, *C. hirusstissima* is not a vine. The petal-like sepals are a common characteristic of buttercups.

ROCK CLEMATIS
Clematis occidentalis
Synonym: *Atragene occidentalis*
Buttercup family (Ranunculaceae)

Description: This plant's 4 nodding, pointed, and veined lavender-blue sepals surround a cluster of white to yellow stamens and styles. The solitary flowers are ¾–2" long and arise singly from the point where the leaves attach to the stem. The opposite, compound leaves have 3 entire to barely toothed leaflets. The long stems are woody vines that climb up bushes and trees. The showy clumps of seeds have feathery tails.

Bloom Season: May to July

Habitat/Range: Found in the shade of spruce trees, woods, and forest edges in the foothills, montane, and subalpine ecosystems from Canada to Colorado.

Comments: Also called blue clematis. "Clematis" is an ancient Greek name for various climbing plants. The clematis symbolizes ingenuity, perhaps because of its clever climbing ability. Scott clematis (*Clematis hirsutissima* var. *scottii*) is commonly distributed in the foothills of the Southern Rockies and has purple, leathery flowers and ovate, entire leaflets.

CHRIS KASSAR

NATIONAL PARK SERVICE

TALL LARKSPUR
Delphinium barbeyi
Buttercup family (Ranunculaceae)

Description: Dark purple flowers form a short, dense cluster atop a stout stem. Five large, showy, dark purple sepals form the flower; the top sepal extends back to create a spur. There are 4 tiny central petals, and the upper pair is edged with white. Leaves are palmately divided into 5–7 toothed lobes. The large, smooth leaves are found primarily on the stem, with few basal leaves. Several sticky, hairy stems can grow 3–6' tall and arise from a single rootstock.

Bloom Season: July and August

Habitat/Range: Grows in groups along stream banks and in wet areas and forest openings in the subalpine and alpine ecosystems. Found in Utah, Colorado, New Mexico, and Arizona.

Comments: Also called subalpine larkspur. *Delphinium* is from the Latin *delphinus* or "dolphin," referring to the resemblance of the flower buds to dolphins. Some botanists place this species in the Hellebore family (Helleboraceae).

DWARF LARKSPUR
Delphinium nuttallianum
Buttercup family (Ranunculaceae)

Description: An open cluster of 4–10 bright purplish-blue flowers arises from a stalk that lacks sticky hairs. Five showy sepals form flowers about 1" across and ½–¾" long. One sepal forms a conspicuous rear spur helpful in identification. Four tiny petals are blue or white with blue markings. The leaves are 3" wide and palmately divided into slender lobes. Stem leaves are alternate and few. The stems usually are single and unbranched. Plants often grow in masses and extend 6–20" tall from a tuber-like root.

Bloom Season: March to July

Habitat/Range: Found on dry, sunny hillsides and beneath ponderosa pines in the foothills and montane ecosystems from Canada to Colorado.

Comments: Also called Nelson's larkspur. Similar species include the taller mountain larkspur (*D. ramosum*), which has small flowers and several stems. Subalpine larkspur (*D. barberyi*) has sticky hairy stems, and its flowers form short, dense clusters. Some botanists place this species in the Hellebore family (Helleboraceae).

CHRIS KASSAR

CHRIS KASSAR

PASQUEFLOWER

Pulsatilla patens ssp. *multifida*
Synonyms: *P.ludoviciana, Anemone patens*
Buttercup family (Ranunculaceae)

Description: This dainty lavender flower is one of the first to open in the spring. The cup-shaped blossom is 1–2" across with 5–7 sepals. The delicately colored sepals have soft hairs on the outer surface. Many bright yellow stamens add a touch of color to the center of the flower. The hairy flower stem bears 1 blossom with leaves to protect the bud. Additional lobed leaves appear at the plant's base once blooming is completed. The stem may grow to 16". The numerous seeds bear feathery tails.

Bloom Season: March to June

Habitat/Range: Found in meadows and open forests in the foothills, montane, and subalpine ecosystems from Alaska to Texas.

Comments: An alternate common name is anemone, based on the Greek word for "wind." *Pasque* is French for Easter, possibly referring to the fact that this plant blooms as soon as snow melts, often around Easter.

BLUE VIOLET

Viola adunca
Violet family (Violaceae)

Description: Like other violets, these flowers look like small pansies, with 2 petals above and 3 below. The united lower petals form a spur. Blossoms are blue or violet, the throat is white with dark lines, and side petals have hairs on the inside. The flowers are ¼–¾" long and attached singly on a slender stalk. Leaves are ¾–1½" long, roundish, and often hairy. The leafy stems may be up to 4" tall.

Bloom Season: April to August

Habitat/Range: Common in moist areas such as aspen groves, streamsides, and edges of fields. Found in the foothills, montane, and subalpine ecosystems from Canada to New Mexico.

Comments: Also called hook violet. *Adunca* means "hooked" in Latin and likely refers to the spur at the back of the flower.

GREEN FLOWERS

This section includes broad-leaved plants with tiny, nonshowy flowers, as well as large flowers that are green or have a greenish cast. Because green flowers grade into white flowers, readers looking for green flowers should check the white section as well.

ALPINE NAILWORT
Paronychia pulvinata
Pink family (Caryophyllaceae)

Description: Light yellowish-green, stalkless flowers are embedded in a tight mat of low vegetation. The inconspicuous blossoms lack petals but have 5 sepals with tiny awns on their tips, 5 stamens topped with yellow pollen, and papery bracts. Thick spine-tipped leaves are less than ¼" long, more long than wide, and have thin silvery stipules. The base of the stem is woody. This ground-hugging perennial grows less than 2" tall.

Bloom Season: May to August

Habitat/Range: Rocky or gravelly slopes, scree fields, and ridges of the alpine tundra from Wyoming to New Mexico.

Comments: Formerly known by the scientific name *P. sessiliflora*, this plant was used to cure infections around the fingernails and toenails, hence its common name, nailwort.

ONE-SIDED WINTERGREEN
Orthilia secunda
Synonyms: *Orthilia obtustata, Pyrola secunda*
Heath family (Ericaceae)

Description: From 4–20 white or greenish-white flowers hang on one side of a slender, often arched stem. The bell-shaped blossoms have 5 petals, 10 stamens, and a straight style that protrudes. The flowers are ¼" long and ¼" across. Shiny, ovate, evergreen leaves are ⅜–2½" long on short stalks. The leaves have slightly toothed edges and appear to be basal but actually grow on the lower ¹⁄₁₀–½" of the stem. This commonly found perennial often grows in groups and reaches 2–10" tall.

Bloom Season: June to August

Habitat/Range: Found in coniferous forests and near streams in the foothills, montane, and subalpine ecosystems from Alaska to New Mexico.

Comments: Also called side bells. *Ortho* means "straight" in Greek, referring to the style, and *secunda* means "side-flowering." Formerly in the Wintergreen family (Pyrolaceae).

CHRIS KASSAR

GREENFLOWER PYROLA
Pyrola chlorantha
Heath family (Ericaceae)

Description: The 3–10 nodding, greenish-white flowers hang from a single, erect, slender, reddish stem. The blossoms are ⅜–⅝" wide and have 5 petals, 10 stamens, and a curved style that sticks out. The leathery, oval to round evergreen leaves are ⅜–1½" long, have small round teeth, and form small basal rosettes. This perennial grows 4–12" tall.

Bloom Season: June to August

Habitat/Range: Moist forests and dry, shaded areas of the foothills, montane, and subalpine ecosystems from the Yukon to New Mexico.

Comments: Also called shinleaf because the leaves were used as a poultice to lessen the pain of bruised shins. That active ingredient in wintergreen leaves is methyl salicylate, a compound similar to aspirin that acts as a natural painkiller. The leaves can be chewed, brewed into a tea, or applied to wounds as a poultice to relieve overall pain, soothe muscles, and ease headaches. *Chlorantha* means "green flowered." Formerly in the Wintergreen family (Pyrolaceae).

43

NATIONAL PARK SERVICE

MONUMENT PLANT
Frasera speciosa
Gentian family (Gentianaceae)

Description: Star-shaped, yellow-green flowers cover the upper portion of a tall, stout stalk that emerges from a large basal rosette. Blossoms have 4 stamens and 4 pointed petals joined at the base, spotted with purple and fringed with hairs. The 1–1½" wide flowers grow on short stalks where the leaves meet the stem. Large oblong to lance-shaped leaves attach to the stem in evenly spaced whorls and get smaller toward the top of the stem. This species can grow 1–7' tall.

Bloom Season: June to August

Habitat/Range: Found in meadows, pine forests, and on hillsides in the foothills, montane, and subalpine ecosystems from Montana to Mexico.

Comments: Also called green gentian, elkweed (elk eat the leaves), or deer's ears (for the shape of the basal leaves). Previously scientists thought this plant was biennial, meaning it flowered in its 2nd season of growth and then died. However, continuous research by Dr. David Inouye at the Rocky Mountain Biological Laboratory in Gothic, Colorado, indicates that monument plant produces flowers only once in its lifetime of 20–80 years and then dies. It is thus called a monocarpic plant, that is, one that grows many years, flowers once, and then dies. Perhaps the most well-known monocarpic plant is the Southwest's century plant. (Information provided by Al Schneider, www.swcoloradowildflowers.com.)

NATIONAL PARK SERVICE

SCOTT F. SMITH

HEARTLEAF TWAYBLADE
Neottia cordata
Synonym: *Listera cordata*
Orchid family (Orchidaceae)

Description: Small, spurless, greenish, whitish, or purplish flowers are arranged in a loose raceme. The long lower lip is cut into 2 narrow pointed segments. Each segment typically bears a tooth near the base at the outside edge. This plant has only 2 opposite, heart-shaped, stalkless leaves located at the middle of the 3–10" stem.

Bloom Season: June to August

Habitat/Range: Found in shaded, moist coniferous or coniferous-hardwood forests and along streams in the montane and subalpine ecosystems from Alaska to New Mexico.

Comments: The common name, referring to the plant's 2 leaves, comes from the English word *tway*, which means "two," and *blade*, meaning "leaf." *Neottia* is Greek for "bird's nest" and refers to the plant's root system—a short rhizome with multiple roots—that resembles a bird's nest. *Cord* means "heart" in Latin.

NORTHERN GREEN BOG ORCHID
Platanthera aquilonis
Synonyms: *Limnorchis hyperborea, Habenaria hyperborea*
Orchid family (Orchidaceae)

Description: A stout stem supports a dense spike of greenish flowers and bracts. The petals and sepals look alike. The 3 sepals form a hood at the top of the blossom. Two petals stick out to the sides, and the bottom petal forms a lip less than ¼" long, with the narrow spur about the same length as the flower lip. The petals may be tinged reddish purple. The lance-shaped leaves have parallel veins and are 2–6" long. This plant usually grows 1–2' tall.

Bloom Season: May to August

Habitat/Range: Seen along streams, in wet meadows, and forests of the foothills, montane, and subalpine ecosystems from Alaska to Colorado.

Comments: The specific name *aquilonis* means "of the north" and refers to its range; it is found across the entire northern United States and up into Canada. The closely related green bog orchid *(P. stricta)* has a spur that is much shorter than the lip of the flower and is found in Utah, Wyoming, and states and territories north to Alaska.

CHRIS KASSAR

GIANT LOUSEWORT
Pedicularis procera
Broomrape family (Orobanchaceae)

Description: Greenish or light yellow flowers with red or purple streaks are interspersed with pointy green bracts. The blossoms are 1–1½" long. The curved upper petal almost touches the wide lower lip. Both basal and stem leaves are pinnately divided into toothed lobes. The fernlike leaves are 8–23" long. The stout stem of this perennial grows 2–4' tall.

Bloom Season: July to September

Habitat/Range: Common in forests and meadows of the montane and subalpine ecosystems from Wyoming to New Mexico.

Comments: Also called Gray's fernleaf lousewort. The specific name *procera* means "very tall." Infusions and tinctures made from a variety of *Pedicularis* species have been used to treat many maladies, including insomnia, joint and muscle pain, muscle spasms, and sprains. Formerly in the Figwort family (Scrophulariaceae).

BARRY BRECKLING

WILLOW DOCK
Rumex triangulivalvis
Synonyms: *R.salicifolius, R.mexicanus*
Buckwheat family (Polygonaceae)

Description: A stout, branched stem supports clusters of small, greenish flowers that often have tinges of red or brown. Blossoms have 6 tepals; the inner 3 are the largest, broadly triangular, and usually have central tubercles. Blooms appear in 4–12" branched clusters of 10–25 flowers near the top of the stem. Light green leaves are flat, smooth, linear-lanceolate, and 5 times as long as they are wide. This plant grows up to 40" tall.

Bloom Season: May to August

Habitat/Range: Grows in disturbed areas, including roadsides, cultivated fields, and moist open ground in plains, foothills, and montane ecosystems from the Yukon to New Mexico.

Comments: *Rumex* is the ancient Latin name for docks or sorrels. Young leaves are edible but sour and taste best when boiled. Seeds can be ground into flour or boiled to make a mealy mush. Because the raw plant contains oxalic acid, it can be toxic in large quantities since oxalates interfere with nutrient absorption.

CHRIS KASSAR

FENDLER'S MEADOWRUE
Thalictrum fendleri var. *fendleri*
Buttercup family (Ranunculaceae)

Description: Clusters of greenish-brown flowers sit atop branched stems with highly divided, compound leaves. Flowers have 4 or 5 sepals, lack petals, and are often nodding. Because this plant is dioecious, meaning male and female flowers are separate, some plants (female) have flowers with pistils and no stamens, while others (male) lack pistils but have many golden stamens dangling from purplish filaments. Scalloped, 3-lobed leaves are ½–1½" long, alternate, and delicate. Leafy, erect stems can grow 1–3' tall. Small, dry, 1-seeded fruits (achenes) that are flattened laterally.

Bloom Season: April to July

Habitat/Range: Grows in moist areas, meadows, and woodlands in the foothills, montane, and subalpine zones from Wyoming to New Mexico.

Comments: Some botanists place *Thalictrum* in Thalictraceae (the Meadowrue family). Navajo Indians used a decoction of this plant as ceremonial medicine, while other tribes used it as a cold remedy.

RED AND ORANGE FLOWERS

NATIONAL PARK SERVICE

This section includes red and orange flowers, as well as those with a maroon or brownish cast. Red flowers grade into pink and purple, so readers looking for red flowers should check the pink, blue, and purple sections as well.

SCOTT F. SMITH

NATIONAL PARK SERVICE

STRAWBERRY BLITE
Chenopodium capitatum
Amaranth family (Amaranthaceae)

Description: Tiny, deep red flowers in rounded clusters decorate the smooth stem of this annual. Blossoms lack petals, but fleshy sepals form round, ⅓–⅔" wide heads to create flowers that resemble tiny strawberries. Smooth green, alternate leaves shaped like arrowheads may be toothless or bear coarse teeth. Stems are hairless, usually branched, and grow 4–24" in height.

Bloom Season: June to August

Habitat/Range: Found in moist, disturbed ground along roads, in burned areas, and near abandoned buildings. It grows in the foothills, montane, and subalpine ecosystems from Alaska to New Mexico.

Comments: Also called Indian paint. The leaves and flowers are edible and high in calcium, vitamins, and protein, but they should be eaten in moderation because they contain saponins and oxalates. Natives used the blood-red blossoms to make ink and dyes. Formerly in the Goosefoot family (Chenopodiaceae).

MOUNTAIN DANDELION
Agoseris aurantiaca
Aster family (Asteraceae)

Description: These 1" wide flowers look like a dandelion that was dipped in deep orange to brownish-red paint. As the blossoms dry, they turn pink or purple. Each leafless stalk bears 1 flower head that has only ray flowers. Several overlapping rows of bracts sit below the flowers. The basal, lance-shaped leaves are 2–14" long and may be entire or toothed. The narrow leaves and stem both have a milky sap. The stems may be 4–24" tall.

Bloom Season: June to September

Habitat/Range: Adds color to meadows and openings in coniferous woods. Found in the foothills, montane, subalpine, and alpine ecosystems from Canada to New Mexico.

Comments: Also called burnt-orange false dandelion and orange agoseris. *Agoseris* means "like a potherb" (a leafy cooked vegetable), referring to the fact that the leaves make delicious cooked or uncooked greens. In Latin, *aurantiaca* means "orange," even though flower color can vary from orange to coppery orange to lavender to the very rare pink.

CHRIS KASSAR

MARY DUBLER

KING'S CROWN

Rhodiola integrifolia
Synonyms: *Sedum rosea, Tolmachevia integrifolia*
Stonecrop family (Crassulaceae)

Description: A flat-topped cluster of deep red to maroon flowers sits atop a succulent, leafy stalk. The 4 or 5 pointed petals are ⅛–½" long. Numerous smooth, fleshy leaves are ⅜–1" long. The alternate leaves are flat with an oblong shape and are ungrooved. Clustered, unbranched stems are 2–12" tall.

Bloom Season: June to August

Habitat/Range: Found in moist or gravelly meadows and open, rocky slopes in the subalpine and alpine ecosystems from Alaska to New Mexico.

Comments: Also called roseroot. Juicy leaves can provide water in an emergency, while both leaves and shoots provide a tasty, vitamin-packed snack when eaten raw or cooked. The plant looks similar to rose crown (*R. rhodantha*), which has flowers ranging from deep pink to light pink to whitish. *R. rhodantha*'s flower cluster forms a rounded column, whereas *R. integrifolia*'s inflorescence is flat.

PINEDROPS

Pterospora andromedea
Heath family (Ericaceae)

Description: This plant lacks chlorophyll, the photosynthetic pigment that gives plants their green color. A raceme of bell-shaped flowers dangles from a slender, conspicuous, reddish-brown stem. The blossoms have 5 pale-yellow lobes, 5 red sepals, and 10 stamens. The scalelike leaves are ¼–1" long. Sticky hairs cover the stout, unbranched stem. The plants grow 1–3' tall. Clusters of dried stems persist into the winter.

Bloom Season: June to August

Habitat/Range: Grows on the forest floor, particularly under conifers in the foothills and montane ecosystems from Canada to New Mexico.

Comments: This parasitic plant lives in association with fungi that break down dead vegetation. *Pterospora* is Greek for "winged seeds," referring to the wing on each seed that carries it to a new spot, aiding in perpetuation of the species. Formerly in the Pinesap family (Monotropaceae).

CHRISTINA MACLEOD

WOOD LILY
Lilium philadelphicum
Lily family (Liliaceae)

Description: These large, showy blossoms have 6 orange-red tepals. The tepals are 2–2½" long and bear dark spots at their bases. Usually, 1–3 flowers top each stem. The smooth leaves have parallel veins. The top leaves are arranged in a whorl, and the rest of the leaves are alternate. Stems arise from bulbs and may be 11–24" tall. Fruits are cylindrical capsules.

Bloom Season: June to August

Habitat/Range: Rare overall, but abundant locally in certain spots. Found on hillsides and in open woods in the foothills to upper montane ecosystems from Canada to New Mexico.

Comments: Also called tiger lily. The colorful blossoms often attract butterflies and hummingbirds.

SCOTT F. SMITH

SCOTT F. SMITH

SPOTTED CORALROOT
Corallorhiza maculata
Orchid family (Orchidaceae)

Description: Loose racemes of up to 30 flowers hang from stout purple, red, or brown stems. The flowers, made up of 3 brownish-purple sepals and 2 similarly colored, lanceolate upper petals, which spread upward and out to the side like wings, grow to ¾" long. The 2-lobed lower lip petal is white and spotted with purple. Reduced leaves appear as thin sheaths on the unbranched, fleshy stem that grows 6–24" in height. This plant often grows in clumps.

Bloom Season: May to August

Habitat/Range: Fairly common in shady, moist forests in the foothills and montane ecosystems from Canada to New Mexico.

Comments: Coralroots are parasitic; they use their roots to feed off fungi on the forest floor and the roots of other plants. People have brewed *C. maculata*'s rhizome—the elongate subterranean stem—into a tea to reduce fevers and act as a sedative. Although usually maroon, yellow albino plants have also been found. Striped coralroot (*C. striata*) looks similar, but its flower is striped instead of spotted.

BROWNIE LADYSLIPPER
Cypripedium fasciculatum
Orchid family (Orchidaceae)

Description: The bottom petal of this unusual flower forms a yellowish-green sac with reddish-brown or dark purple markings. The other 2 petals and brownish-purple sepals look alike, but the bottom 2 sepals are united. Usually, 2–4 drooping flowers, each measuring 1–1½" long, are found on every stem. There are 2 opposite, roundish leaves that are 2–6" long. The plants often grow in clusters 2–8" tall.

Bloom Season: April to August

Habitat/Range: Relatively rare, the plant grows in coniferous forests and on hillsides in the montane and subalpine ecosystems from Canada to Colorado.

Comments: Also called clustered ladyslipper. Many ladyslippers are rare as they have very specific habitat requirements. The name *Cypripedium* means "Venus slipper." Some botanists place this species in the Ladyslipper family (Cypripediaceae).

CHRIS KASSAR

NATIONAL PARK SERVICE

WYOMING PAINTBRUSH
Castilleja linariifolia
Broomrape family (Orobanchaceae)

Description: Like other paintbrushes, the colorful part of the plant consists of bracts and sepals. A cluster of bright red, deeply lobed bracts and yellowish-green flowers (tubes that extend beyond the red bracts), grows atop a slender stem. The hairy, red sepals have a deep slit on one side. The red-tinged, green corolla is 2-lipped and more than 1" long. Alternate leaves are very narrow and entire or with lobes. The leaves have 1 main vein and are 1½–4" long. This perennial grows 1–4' tall and may be branched or unbranched.

Bloom Season: June to September

Habitat/Range: Commonly found growing on rocky hillsides, among shrubs, and in meadows and open forests in the foothills and montane ecosystems from Wyoming to New Mexico.

Comments: Also called narrowleaf paintbrush. This is the state flower of Wyoming. Many kinds of paintbrush are partially parisitic on the roots of other plants such as sage *(Artemesia)*. Formerly in the Figwort family (Scrophulariaceae).

SCARLET PAINTBRUSH
Castilleja miniata
Broomrape family (Orobanchaceae)

Description: Consistent with paintbrush characteristics, bracts and sepals make up the colorful part of this plant. A dense cluster of showy, toothed, bright red to scarlet bracts and tubular greenish flowers grow atop a branched stem. The colored bracts typically have 3 deep lobes, and the green corolla is 2-lipped, inconspicuous, and less than 1½" long. Alternate leaves have 3 main veins and are 1–4" long. The leaves are entire, or the upper leaves may be lobed. Grows 1–3' tall.

Bloom Season: May to September

Habitat/Range: Common in moist meadows, open woods, and among shrubs in the foothills and montane ecosystems from Canada to New Mexico.

Comments: Also called giant red paintbrush. Can be confused with *C. linariifolia*, which also has red bracts; however its calyx has a deep cut in the front and a shallow cut in the back, whereas *C. miniata* has an equally deep cut between the 2 sides. Foothills paintbrush (*C. integra*) is a common orange-bracted variety. Formerly in the Figwort family (Scrophulariaceae).

CHRIS KASSAR

CHRIS KASSAR

SCARLET GILIA

Ipomopsis aggregata
Synonym: *Gilia aggregata*
Phlox family (Polemoniaceae)

Description: Showy, long clusters of red to pink, trumpet-shaped flowers hang along slender stems. The flowers are ¾–2" long, have 5 pointed lobes, stamens, and anthers that extend beyond the flower's throat. Alternate, pinnately divided leaves are 1–2" long, narrow, sticky, and get smaller near the top of the stem. This common and widespread biennial often grows in groups and varies in height from 6–84" tall.

Bloom Season: May to September

Habitat/Range: Common in dry fields, open forests, on gravelly slopes, and along roads in the foothills and montane ecosystems from Montana to New Mexico.

Comments: Also called fairy trumpets or skyrocket gilia. This species was first described from a specimen collected by Meriwether Lewis during the Lewis and Clark expedition.

ALPINE SORREL

Oxyria digyna
Buckwheat family (Polygonaceae)

Description: Numerous tiny flowers varying from light green to reddish dangle in tight clusters at the top of a hairless stem. The ¹⁄₁₆" long flowers lack petals but have green or red sepals with 4 lobes. The mainly basal leaves are kidney shaped and entire. The fleshy, long-stalked leaves are smooth and up to 1" in diameter. The small, reddish fruits are round and winged. A simple stem usually is 2–12" tall, but can reach up to 2' at times.

Bloom Season: June to September

Habitat/Range: Found in moist, open rocky areas, including spots beneath and between boulders in the montane, subalpine, and alpine ecosystems from Alaska to New Mexico.

Comments: The name *Oxyria* is derived from a Greek word meaning "sour." It refers to the taste of the leaves, which are high in oxalate and vitamin C. The young greens make a thirst-quenching snack and add life to salads and dressings. They can also be added to casseroles or dried and sprinkled on grains for added flavor. It is best to consume only small amounts, to stick with the young leaves, and to boil or dry the leaves before eating because they contain oxalates, which can be toxic in large quantities.

NATIONAL PARK SERVICE BY RUSSELL SMITH

RED COLUMBINE
Aquilegia elegantula
Buttercup family (Ranunculaceae)

Description: These beautiful flowers have 5 red, petal-like sepals and 5 yellow, funnel-shaped petals with red spurs. The drooping blossoms are 1–2" long with many yellow stamens that protrude from the flower. Leaves are mainly basal and smooth. The compound leaves are divided into 3 segments, each segment being 3-lobed. Slender stems are 4–24" tall.

Bloom Season: May to August

Habitat/Range: Found in moist areas, open woods, hillsides, and along streams in the upper foothills, montane, and subalpine ecosystems of Utah, New Mexico, Colorado, and Arizona.

Comments: This plant looks much like the larger crimson columbine (*A. formosa*), found from Alaska to Utah. In Latin, *aquila* means "eagle," which could refer to the similarities shared between the spurs of the flower and the talons of an eagle. William Weber, renowned botanist and author of *Colorado Flora,* writes that the word originates from *aqua* ("water") and *legere* ("to collect"), referring to the "nectar at the base of the spur."

PINK FLOWERS

This section includes flowers grading from pale pinkish white to vivid electric pink and rose purple. Because pink flowers grade into white and purple flowers, readers looking for pink flowers should check the blue, purple, and white sections as well.

CHRIS KASSAR

NODDING ONION
Allium cernuum
Onion family (Alliaceae)

Description: Onions usually have flower parts in multiples of 3 and leaves with parallel veins. An umbel or nodding cluster of flowers is a distinctive characteristic of this species. Flowers are bell shaped and have stamens that stick out past the 6 small ovate, pink or white tepals. Two papery bracts usually cover the buds and fall off by the time the flowers bloom. Grasslike basal leaves are 2–10" long, and the leafless flower stalk grows 4–24" tall. The edible bulbs and the rest of the foliage have the typical scent of onions.

Bloom Season: June to October

Habitat/Range: Found in moist soils, grassy fields, and slopes in the foothills, montane, and subalpine ecosystems from Canada to New Mexico.

Comments: *A.cernuum* is the most widespread North American species of the genus. Similar in color, height, and range to Geyer's onion (*A. geyeri*), but that species does not flower in a nodding umbel; *A. geyeri* blooms in an erect cluster and has stamens that do not stick out past the small petals and sepals. In North America, scientists discovered evidence of indigenous people using wild onions as food 6,000 years ago. Native Americans ate the young leaves and bulbs raw or cooked. Explorers from both Stephen Long's and Prince Maximilian's 19th-century expeditions ate wild onion leaves to cure an illness that probably was scurvy. Formerly in the Lily family (Liliaceae).

DENVER BOTANIC GARDENS

AL SCHNEIDER, WWW.SWCOLORADOWILDFLOWERS.COM

SHOWY MILKWEED
Asclepias speciosa
Dogbane family (Apocynaceae)

Description: This hairy, grayish plant's star-shaped, baseball-sized clusters of pink or whitish flowers are hard to miss. The ¾" wide blossoms have 5 sepals, 5 bent-down petals, and 5 curved, horned hoods that look like petals. Simple 3–8" long leaves are lance shaped, ovate, or oblong. The thick, opposite leaves have short stalks and obvious veins. After fertilization, pods grow to 2–4½" long. Short white hairs cover the pods that split open to release plumed brown seeds. Stems with milky sap grow 1–5' tall.

Bloom Season: June to August

Habitat/Range: Found in meadows, open woods, roadside fields, sunny and dry environs, and in disturbed areas from the foothills to montane ecosystems from Canada to Arizona.

Comments: Also called pink or common milkweed. The striped black, yellow, and white caterpillars of monarch butterflies feed on milkweed foliage. For generations, Native Americans have used this plant for fiber, food, and medicine. Some milkweeds are highly poisonous; milkweed sap contains toxic chemicals that can cause vomiting or death if ingested in high doses. Formerly in the Milkweed family (Asclepiadaceae).

ROSY PUSSYTOES
Antennaria rosea
Synonym: *A. microphylla*
Aster family (Asteraceae)

Description: Flower heads that look and feel like the pads of a cat's paw give this plant its common name. Heads contain only disk flowers and are less than ¼" tall. The bracts around the flower heads usually are pink or sometimes whitish. Primarily basal leaves are up to ¾" long with woolly hairs. The leaves are rounded at the tip and narrow toward the base. The light gray-green vegetation spreads by runners to form mats. Stems are 8–16" tall.

Bloom Season: May to August

Habitat/Range: Commonly found in moderately dry areas, meadows, and open woods in the foothills, montane, subalpine, and alpine ecosystems from Alaska to New Mexico.

Comments: One plant usually has all male flowers or all female flowers. Telling *Antennaria* species apart is complex because of hybridization and the fact that some colonies contain only male or female plants while other colonies contain both. *Antennaria* refers to floral parts that resemble antennae.

AL SCHNEIDER, WWW.SWCOLORADOWILDFLOWERS.COM

NATIONAL PARK SERVICE

BEAUTIFUL DAISY
Erigeron elatior
Aster family (Asteraceae)

Description: Numerous narrow ray flowers are lavender or pink and surround a yellow center. There are 1–3 nodding heads per stem. Bracts around the flower heads are about equal in length, with pink, woolly hairs. The simple, entire leaves are lance shaped and more than ¾" wide. Upper leaves clasp the stem. The leafy stems are extremely hairy and may be up to 24" tall. This perennial plant often grows in eye-catching colonies.

Bloom Season: July to September

Habitat/Range: Found in meadows, along streams, and other moist areas in the montane and subalpine ecosystems of Wyoming, Colorado, Utah, and New Mexico.

Comments: Also called pink daisy or tall fleabane. In Latin, *elatior* means "tall."

DOTTED BLAZING STAR
Liatris punctata
Aster family (Asteraceae)

Description: Slim, elongated clusters of showy pink to lavender blossoms brighten meadows in late summer. Each flower head contains 3–8 disk flowers with threadlike stigmas that give the bloom a feathery look. Overlapping bracts surround the many flowers that grow in crowded, narrow spikes atop a hairless stem. Leaves are very narrow, 3–6" long, and have tiny dots on the underside. The clustered, unbranched stems may be 6–32" tall. Seeds have feathery bristles.

Bloom Season: July to October

Habitat/Range: Dry meadows in the foothills and montane ecosystems from Canada to New Mexico.

Comments: Also called Kansas gayfeather, dotted gayfeather, or snakeroot. *Liatris* roots contain inulin, a mild kidney and liver tonic. Tribes mashed roots to treat snake bites, simmered roots to make cough syrups, and used tea to ease throat inflammation and kidney and bladder problems.

NATIONAL PARK SERVICE BY RUSSELL SMITH

CHRIS KASSAR

MOUNTAIN BALL CACTUS
Pediocactus simpsonii
Cactus family (Cactaceae)

Description: Beautiful magenta, pink, white, or yellow flowers top this small ball-shaped cactus. The fragrant flowers have many pointed petals and numerous stamens. Cactus spines are modified leaves; this species has 5–11 brown central spines surrounded by 15–30 white spines. Fleshy stems are 2–3" wide with projections called tubercles that lack grooves on the upper side. This plant grows 1–8" tall.

Bloom Season: March to July

Habitat/Range: Found in dry, sandy soil of meadows, pinyon-juniper woodlands, sagebrush, and sunny pine forests in the foothills and montane ecosystems from Montana to New Mexico.

Comments: *P. simpsonii* is extremely variable. It is the most widely distributed of any *Pediocactus* and grows at the highest elevation. The similar ball cactus (*Escobaria vivipara* var. *vivipara*) has a groove on one side of each tubercle. Hen-and-chickens cactus (*Echinocereus viridiflorus*) has greenish-yellow flowers.

MOSS CAMPION
Silene acaulis var. *subacaulescens*
Pink family (Caryophyllaceae)

Description: Numerous tiny flowers form a mass of pink, lavender, and occasionally whitish blossoms on a pincushion cluster of leaves. The flower's 5 petals have a small notch at the tip. The ¼" wide, tubular flowers have such a short stalk that the blossoms barely rise above the tiny leaves. The opposite, pointed leaves are ¼–½" long, opposite and very narrow. This circumboreal, evergreen perennial forms a mosslike mat of vegetation that may reach 1' across and 1–2½" tall.

Bloom Season: June to August

Habitat/Range: A pioneer species in windy, rocky sites on alpine tundra from Canada to New Mexico.

Comments: In the 1950s, Robert Griggs extensively studied *S. acaulis* in Rocky Mountain National Park. He found that plants grew "fairly rapidly," reaching 10" in diameter in about 20 years and reported that Europe's cushions of 20" across may be 100 years old. *Acaulis* is a common specific name meaning "without stem." (Information provided by Al Schneider, www.swcoloradowildflowers.com.)

CHRIS KASSAR

NATIONAL PARK SERVICE

ROCKY MOUNTAIN BEEPLANT
Peritoma serrulata
Synonym: *Cleome serrulata*
Cleome family (Cleomaceae)

Description: A cluster of pink to lavender—or occasionally white—4-petaled flower blooms sit atop a branched stem. The showy flowers are cross shaped and have 6 protruding stamens. Alternate, compound leaves divide into 3 lance-shaped leaflets. Long, narrow green seedpods dangle below flowers. This annual can grown 6–60" tall.

Bloom Season: June to August

Habitat/Range: Common in sandy meadows, near roads, and along trails in the foothills and montane ecosystems from Canada to New Mexico.

Comments: Also called pink cleome or stink-weed due to the unpleasant smell of the foliage. Plentiful nectar attracts bees, giving the plant its common name. This was an important food source for Native Americans who cooked the young shoots, leaves, and flowers. Infusions were used to treat stomachaches, and a poultice helped soothe sore eyes. Formerly in the Caper family (Capparidaceae).

QUEEN'S CROWN
Rhodiola rhodantha
Synonyms: *Clementsia rhodantha, Sedum rhodanthum*
Stonecrop family (Crassulaceae)

Description: A long, rounded column crowded with pink or almost white flowers sits atop a succulent, leafy stalk. The 4 or 5 pointed petals are ⅜–½" long, forming a flower cluster 1" wide. Numerous smooth, fleshy, alternate leaves are flat with an oblong shape and are ½–1" long. Clustered, unbranched stems are 6–12" tall.

Bloom Season: June to August

Habitat/Range: Found in wet meadows and near streams, ponds, and marshes in montane, subalpine, and alpine ecosystems from Montana to New Mexico.

Comments: Also called rose crown. Looks similar to king's crown (*R. integrifolia*), which has red flowers, but *R. rhodantha* has a more cylindrical pink head and is found most often in wet, moist areas.

CHRIS KASSAR

KINNIKINNICK
Arctostaphylos uva-ursi
Heath family (Ericaceae)

Description: Tiny urn-shaped flowers dangle in groups from short branches. Waxy white and/or pink blossoms are less than ¼" long and have 5 lobes. Leathery, evergreen leaves are ¼–1" long and alternate. The leaves are entire, ovate, and widest toward the tip. Stems are woody and creeping with peeling, reddish bark. Stem branches have long, sticky hairs. The plant may be up to 6" tall. The fruit is a pea-sized red berry.

Bloom Season: March to July

Habitat/Range: Forms a ground cover under evergreen forests or in open areas in the foothills, montane, subalpine, and alpine ecosystems from Alaska to New Mexico.

Comments: Also called bearberry. In Greek, *arctos* means "bear," and *staphyle* means "grape," while *uva* means "grape," and *ursus* means "bear." Bears, along with a host of other animals, enjoy feasting on this berry. Deer and bighorn sheep also browse on the evergreen leaves and twigs in winter. Native Americans smoked the dried leaves of kinnikinnick on their own or mixed with tobacco. When cooked slowly, the bland berries pop like popcorn.

NATIONAL PARK SERVICE

BOG LAUREL
Kalmia microphylla
Heath family (Ericaceae)

Description: Clusters of deep pink, cup-shaped flowers are ⅜–¾" across. The blossoms have 5 lobes and 10 stamens. The opposite, evergreen leaves are dark green above with light-colored hairs below. The simple, ¼–1½" long leaves are entire, with the edges often rolled under. Woody, branched stems of this evergreen shrub are 4–18" tall and form low-spreading mats over the ground.

Bloom Season: April to July

Habitat/Range: Uncommon, but may be profuse at the edges of streams and ponds and in wet areas in the subalpine and alpine ecosystems. Found from Canada to Colorado.

Comments: Also called swamp or alpine laurel. Small pouches protect the pollen-bearing anthers until maturity. The weight of an insect or expansion of the flower releases the anthers.

CHRIS KASSAR

NATIONAL PARK SERVICE

BOG PYROLA

Pyrola asarifolia ssp. *asarifolia*
Synonym: *P. rotundifolia* ssp.*asarifolia*
Heath family (Ericaceae)

Description: Nodding pink to rose-purple waxy flowers grow in a tall raceme. Each blossom is less than ½" across and has 5 petals, 10 stamens, and a long, curved style. Roundish leaves are basal or located near the base of the stem. The stalked, leathery leaves are green above and brownish below. The leaves may be up to 3½" long with tiny rounded teeth. This plant can grow to 16" tall.

Bloom Season: June to August

Habitat/Range: Wet, shady ground of streamsides, bogs, springs, and coniferous forests in the foothills, montane, and subalpine ecosystems from Alaska to New Mexico.

Comments: Also called pink pyrola or swamp wintergreen. *Asarifolia* comes from the Latin *asarum* ("ginger") and *folium* ("leaf"), referring to the similarities shared between the leaves of this plant and wild ginger (*Asarum* spp.). Formerly in the Wintergreen family (Pyrolaceae).

COLORADO LOCO

Oxytropis lambertii
Bean family (Fabaceae)

Description: Like all loco flowers, these blossoms are pealike, with the tip of the keel pointed. Brilliant, ½–1" long magenta flowers cluster in tight groups atop a leafless stalk. The sepals and beanlike fruit have white hairs. Leaves are pinnately compound with 7–17 leaflets covered with silvery hairs. The plants are 4–16" in height.

Bloom Season: April to August

Habitat/Range: Common in fields in the foothills, montane, and subalpine ecosystems from Canada to New Mexico.

Comments: Also called Lambert's crazyweed or purple locoweed, this plant turns some meadows into seas of magenta. It may hybridize with Rocky Mountain loco (*O. sericea*) to produce whitish-lavender flowers and may be confused with Parry's loco (*O. parryi*), which is a shorter, more sparsely flowered alpine variety.

NATIONAL PARK SERVICE

FEWFLOWER LOCO
Oxytropis multiceps
Bean family (Fabaceae)

Description: As its common name implies, there are only 1–4 flowers on each short stalk. Like all loco flowers, these blossoms are pealike and the top of the keel is pointed. The ½–1" long flowers are rose pink or purple with pink sepals that inflate to enclose the ripe fruit. Pinnately compound leaves have 5–9 leaflets covered with gray hairs. The ¾–4" plant grows in clumps.

Bloom Season: May to August

Habitat/Range: Dry, gravelly slopes in the foothills, montane, and subalpine ecosystems in Colorado, Utah, and Wyoming.

Comments: Also called tufted loco. Many loco-weeds (*Oxytropis* spp.) are poisonous to horses and cattle. Some can cause severe damage or even death, and usually these animals only eat locoweed if better forage is unavailable. After eating quantities of the plant, the animals act crazily, hence the name.

NATIONAL PARK SERVICE

SHOWY LOCOWEED
Oxytropis splendens
Bean family (Fabaceae)

Description: Numerous rose-pink, dark blue, or purple flowers are bunched in woolly clusters atop a stem covered in silky white hairs. The ¼–½" long blossoms occasionally are white with purple on the tip of the keel. Like all loco flowers, these blossoms are pealike, with the tip of the keel pointed. Both sepals and pods have white hairs. Basal leaves are pinnately compound, while clusters of 2–4 tiny lanceolate leaflets are arranged in whorls around the stem. The plants grow 4–14" tall.

Bloom Season: June to August

Habitat/Range: Common in dry, rocky meadows and aspen groves in the montane and subalpine ecosystems from Canada to New Mexico.

Comments: Also called whorled loco, this plant can be toxic and sometimes fatal to animals if eaten.

NATIONAL PARK SERVICE

CHRIS KASSAR

ALPINE CLOVER
Trifolium dasyphyllum
Bean family (Fabaceae)

Description: The top petal of these ⅜–¾" long flowers is white or cream colored. The other petals are pink or purple. Typically, 10–30 pealike blossoms are borne in a rounded cluster atop a leafless stem. Under the flower head are green-and-white bracts. The basal leaves have 3 very narrow, folded leaflets that are less than 1" long. The leaflets are entire and very hairy, particularly on the underside. This mat plant is 1–6" tall and grows in clumps.

Bloom Season: June to August

Habitat/Range: Common in windy, rocky areas of the subalpine and alpine ecosystems from Montana to New Mexico.

Comments: Also called whiproot clover. *Trifolium* means "three leaves," referring to the leaflets, and *dasyphyllum* means "shaggy or hairy plant." Parry clover (*T. parryi*) is a hairless species that grows in moist subalpine and alpine meadows and has 6–20 rose-purple to reddish-purple flowers clustered in each large round head. The low-growing dwarf clover (*T. nanum*) has only 1–4 flowers per head and is very tiny, reaching heights of only 1".

LITTLE GENTIAN
Gentianella amarella ssp. *acuta*
Synonym: *G. acuta*
Gentian family (Gentianaceae)

Description: These ¼–¾" long tubular flowers with fringed throats are often purplish blue, but sometimes pale yellow with tinges of blue. Sepals are joined at the base, and blossoms have 5 pointed lobes with a fringe of hairs inside the flower. Opposite, smooth, broad to narrow lance-shaped leaves are ¼–1½" long and attach directly to a slender stem. The erect, leafy stem may be simple or branched. Plants are 2–16" tall.

Bloom Season: June to September

Habitat/Range: Grows in stream banks and moist meadows in the foothills, montane, subalpine, and alpine ecosystems from Alaska to New Mexico.

Comments: Also called northern gentian. Engelmann gentian (*G. amarella* ssp. *heterosepala*) has sepal lobes of 2 different sizes. The short alpine oneflower gentian (*Comastoma tenellum*) has small blue flowers. For ages, gentian root has been used to treat digestive disorders and chronic disease. *G. amarella* is one of many species whose root has anti-inflammatory and antiseptic properties and agents that can rid the body of worms, increase appetite, and strengthen and tone the stomach and digestive system.

NATIONAL PARK SERVICE

FREMONT GERANIUM
Geranium caespitosum
Geranium family (Geraniaceae)

Description: The 5 pink to lavender petals have purple veins that guide bees to nectar and pollen. The flowers are 1½" wide with long, soft hairs on part of their length. Blossoms have 5 sepals and 10 stamens. Palmately lobed leaves are ¾–3" wide, divided into 3–5 toothed segments, and have rounded lobes. Sticky hairs cover the 4–30" stems, which grow in clusters. The seeds may be up to 1⅛" long.

Bloom Season: May to August

Habitat/Range: Common along forest edges, in dry meadows, and on slopes in the foothills, montane, and subalpine ecosystems from Wyoming to New Mexico.

Comments: Also called purple wild geranium. *Geranium* comes from a Greek word meaning "crane." This refers to the long seeds, which look like a crane's bill. *Caespitosum* means "growing in clumps." The common name honors John Charles Fremont, who collected this and a lot of other plants during his 19th-century western expeditions.

CHRIS KASSAR / INSET CHRISTINA MACLEOD

WAX CURRANT
Ribes cereum
Synonym: *R. inebrians*
Gooseberry family (Grossulariaceae)

Description: Fragrant and tubular pink flowers hang off this shrub in small clusters of 1–8 flowers. The hairy blossoms are about ¼" long and have 5 lobes and protruding styles. Alternate leaves have 3–5 shallow, toothed lobes and are typically less than 1½" wide. This deciduous shrub grows 20–78" tall, has sticky hairs, and lacks thorns. Fleshy reddish-orange berries ripen in midsummer.

Bloom Season: April to August

Habitat/Range: Widespread and common on dry hillsides, near streams, and in woodlands of foothills and montane ecosystems from Canada to New Mexico.

Comments: *Cereum* means "waxy," referring to the waxy secretion of the leaves. *R. cereum* provides a tasty backcountry snack, as do many other species of the genus. Ribes are commonly found throughout montane ecosystems in the region and include what people commonly call gooseberries and currants. The Zunis, Hopis, and other Native Americans collected the berries of this and other currant species. They ate the berries cooked, dried, or raw. Today people mix the currants with sugar to make jam. Bears, rodents, and many species of birds eat these berries, and deer and elk browse the green leaves.

STEVE OLSON

HORSEMINT
Monarda fistulosa ssp. *fistulosa* var. *menthifolia*
Mint family (Lamiaceae)

Description: Many pink to purple tubular, 2-lipped flowers cluster in a rounded head atop a square stem. Upper lip is narrow, lower lip is 3-lobed, and heads measure 1–3" across. Stamens stick out beyond the petals. Under the 1–1½" long showy flowers lie several leafy bracts. The toothed, ovate leaves are fragrant, hairy, and opposite. The typically unbranched stems grow 1–3' tall, and the plant has a strong, minty odor.

Bloom Season: June to August

Habitat/Range: On sunny slopes, along road-sides, and on the edges of aspen forests in the foothills and montane ecosystems from Canada to New Mexico.

Comments: Also called wild bergamot or beebalm because it is a favorite haunt of bees, butterflies, and hummingbirds. Native Americans made tea from the leaves and/or flowers to relieve colds, fevers, stomachaches, the flu, pneumonia, and kidney problems.

JOHN B. NELSON

WOUNDWORT
Stachys pilosa var. *pilosa*
Synonym: *S. palustris* var. *pilosa*
Mint family (Lamiaceae)

Description: White, pink, or lavender 2-lipped flowers appear in several tiers of whorls at the top of a square, hairy stem. There usually are 2–6 flowers in each whorl. Darker spots decorate the bottom lip of the ⅜–⅝" long blossoms. Each flower has 5 sepal lobes and 4 stamens. The toothed, ovate leaves are 1½–3¼" long and hairy. This perennial grows 6–31" tall.

Bloom Season: June to September

Habitat/Range: Moist soil of meadows and streamsides in the foothills and montane ecosystems from Canada to New Mexico.

Comments: Also called swamp or hairy hedge-nettle. People have used this plant to relieve colic, heal wounds, and as a yellow dye.

NATIONAL PARK SERVICE

AL SCHNEIDER, WWW.SWCOLORADOWILDFLOWERS.COM

TWINFLOWER

Linnaea borealis
Twinflower family (Linnaeaceae)

Description: These dainty ½" long, pink or white, bell-shaped flowers have 5 lobes. Two fragrant, paired, nodding blossoms dangle from a forked, leafless stalk that grows no taller than 4". The opposite evergreen leaves are roundish, entire or slightly toothed, and less than 1" long. Its semiwoody, creeping stems lie flat on the ground, forming mats of vegetation.

Bloom Season: June to August

Habitat/Range: Graces moist, shady areas and evergreen forests in the montane and subalpine ecosystems from Alaska to New Mexico.

Comments: *L. borealis* is circumboreal, and 2 other varieties are found in Europe and Asia. The generic name honors Carolus Linnaeus, the Swedish botanist who developed the 2-name system for designating plants and animals and was especially fond of this delicate beauty. The specific name means "northern" in Greek, referring to its distribution across the Northern Hemisphere. Formerly in the Honeysuckle family (Caprifoliaceae).

PURPLE CHECKER MALLOW

Sidalcea neomexicana ssp. *neomexicana*
Mallow family (Malvaceae)

Description: Numerous large, showy, magenta to purple, cup-shaped blossoms grow in a long spike on top of a tall stalk. Flowers have 5 broad, delicate petals and many stamens joined at their base to form a tube around the branched style. This plant has round, lobed basal leaves measuring up to 4" and deeply incised, smaller upper leaves. Basal leaves and stems have numerous silky hairs. This plant often grows in widely spread colonies and can reach up to 3' tall.

Bloom Season: June to August

Habitat/Range: Found in wetlands, marshy areas, and near streams in montane and subalpine ecosystems from Wyoming to Colorado.

Comments: Also called salt spring checkerbloom. The flowers of this plant are bisexual, meaning that both the male and female parts occur in the same flower.

STEVE OLSON

STEVE OLSON

SPRING BEAUTY
Claytonia lanceolata
Candy-Flower family (Montiaceae)

Description: Small 5-petaled, white to pinkish flowers grow atop arching stalks. Blossoms have 2 sepals, and 1 pair of opposite egg- to lance-shaped leaves shoot from each slender stem. An early spring bloomer, this delicate plant has an underground stalk that grows from deeply buried corms. This delicate plant grows 2–8" tall, but part of it remains underground.

Bloom Season: April to July

Habitat/Range: Found in moist soil, often near snowbeds and/or after snowmelt. Widely distributed from foothills to alpine ecosystems from Canada to New Mexico.

Comments: In 1806, Meriwether Lewis collected the first specimens of this plant for science. The Latin *lanceolata* refers to the lancelike leaf shape. *C. lanceolata*'s leaves are a tasty snack containing vitamins A and C, and corms can be eaten raw or cooked. Deer, elk, and Rocky Mountain bighorn sheep enjoy the leaves, while grizzly bears and rodents favor the corms. Formerly in the Purslane family (Portulacaceae).

PYGMY BITTERROOT
Lewisia pygmaea
Synonym: *Oreobroma pygmaeum*
Candy-Flower family (Montiaceae)

Description: Tiny white, pink, or magenta flowers with 5–9 petals and 2 sepals grow on a single stem. Petals are narrowly oblong, pointed at the tips and often have darker pink veins. Basal leaves are simple, fleshy, narrow, linear, and flattened. The 1–3½" leaves curve upward and form a basal rosette that supports this ground hugger. This plant may be less than 1" tall, but it typically grows to 2".

Bloom Season: May to August

Habitat/Range: Found in a variety of habitats including woodlands, meadows, dry slopes, moist areas and tundra in montane, subalpine and alpine zones from Canada to New Mexico.

Comments: This fleshy root is shaped like a carrot and is edible, but the root's outer skin is very bitter. Named in honor of Meriwether Lewis, who collected the first specimen of this genus, *L. rediviva*, in Montana in 1806. Formerly in the Purslane family (Portulacaceae).

CHRIS KASSAR

FIREWEED

Chamaenerion angustifolium ssp. *circumvagum*
Synonyms: *Chamerion danielsii, Epilobium angustifolium*
Evening Primrose family (Onagraceae)

Description: Bright pink to rose-purple flowers grow in showy racemes atop tall, leafy stems. The 4 broad petals form a blossom that is 1" across. Its 4-lobed stigma is a common feature of this family's members. The lowest flowers in the long, crowded raceme bloom first and then form narrow pods 2–3" long. When ripe, the pods open to release tiny, plumed seeds into the wind. Lance-shaped, alternate leaves are 2–6" long with prominent veins. The mainly unbranched stems may grow from 20" to a towering 7' tall.

Bloom Season: June to September

Habitat/Range: Locally abundant in burned areas, along roadsides and streamsides, in disturbed soil, and along forest edges in the foothills, montane, and subalpine ecosystems from Alaska to New Mexico.

Comments: Tea and honey made from the blossoms provides a delectable treat that also helps settle an upset stomache. The young shoots and flowers can be eaten raw or cooked, making a tasty, vitamin-packed addition to salads and stir-fries. Roots mashed into a poultice soothe burns and rashes. Historically, the "fluff" from mature seedpods made the perfect tinder to start campfires for explorers, while Natives rubbed the flowers on mittens to make them waterproof.

CHRIS KASSAR

FAIRY SLIPPER
Calypso bulbosa var. *americana*
Orchid family (Orchidaceae)

Description: This delicate and fragrant rose-purple to pink flower has a slipper-shaped lip, hence its common name. There are 3 sepals and 3 petals, 1 of which forms the whitish-pink, lower slipper-shaped lip that is dappled with purple streaks or spots and yellow hairs. The other 2 petals and 3 sepals are darker pink to purple and look similar. A single, 1¼" nodding flower sits atop a reddish stem. The 2–8" stem has a tubelike sheath around it. One dark green basal leaf often appears after the flower is finished blooming. The ovate leaf is 1¼–2½" long.

Bloom Season: May to June

Habitat/Range: Uncommon, but may be abundant in spots. Grows in moist, shady evergreen forests in the foothills, montane, and subalpine ecosystems from Alaska to New Mexico.

Comments: Also called Venus's slipper or calypso orchid. Some botanists place this species in the Ladyslipper family (Cypripediaceae).

CHRIS KASSAR

ERNIE MARX

ROSY PAINTBRUSH
Castilleja rhexiifolia
Broomrape family (Orobanchaceae)

Description: The hairy sepals and bracts of this species are rose pink, purple, red, or occasionally yellow. The bracts are entire or barely lobed, with the middle segment the largest. The inconspicuous petals are green, and the upper lip much longer than the lower lip. Relatively narrow leaves are 1–2½" long and have 3 main veins. The leaves mostly are entire, but the upper leaves may be 3-lobed. The unbranched stem grows 7–23" tall and is often found in clumps.

Bloom Season: June to September

Habitat/Range: Common in moist meadows, open glades, and on hillsides in the subalpine and alpine ecosystems from Canada to Colorado.

Comments: It can be difficult to differentiate this species from scarlet paintbrush (*C. miniata*), which has consistently scarlet inflorescences. *C. rhexiifolia*'s variation may be due to hybridization with other species including western yellow paintbrush (*C. occidentalis*). Formerly in the Figwort family (Scrophulariaceae).

CLUSTERED BROOMRAPE
Orobanche fasciculata
Synonym: *Aphyllon fasciculatum*
Broomrape family (Orobanchaceae)

Description: This plant usually bears 4–10 stalked pinkish, dull yellow, or light purple flowers. The tubular blossoms are ½–1¼" long and have a 2-lobed upper lip, 3-lobed lower lip, and calyxes that are shorter than the corolla tubes. Alternate leaves are small and scalelike. Thick pinkish stalks are fleshy and covered with sticky hairs. Grows 1–6" tall.

Bloom Season: May to August

Habitat/Range: Found in dry meadows and on hillsides in the foothills and montane ecosystems from Canada to New Mexico.

Comments: Also called tufted broomrape. This perennial lacks chlorophyll and is parasitic on many plants, including the roots of sages (*Artemesia*) and other members of the Aster family (Asteraceae). May be confused with naked broomrape (*O. uniflora*), which shares similar habitat. *O. uniflora* has slender stems without woody bases and flowers with calyx lobes that are longer than the corolla tubes. Typically *O. uniflora* has only 1 flower or, at most, 2–3 flowers.

CHRIS KASSAR

NATIONAL PARK SERVICE

ELEPHANT HEADS
Pedicularis groenlandica
Broomrape family (Orobanchaceae)

Description: These unmistakable pinkish-purple flowers resemble miniature elephant heads with ears and a long, curved trunk. The blossoms are arranged in a spike atop a purple stem. There are both basal and stem leaves. The leaves are fern-like—pinnately divided into leaflets with toothed lobes. Even the 2–10" long leaves have a purplish tinge. The unbranched stems grow 6–28" high.

Bloom Season: June to August

Habitat/Range: Common in bogs, wet meadows, and near streams and ponds; found in the montane, subalpine, and alpine ecosystems from Alaska to New Mexico.

Comments: Also called elephantella. *Groenlandica* refers to Greenland since the 1st specimen ever identified was collected there.

BEARDED SIDEBELLS PENSTEMON
Penstemon secundiflorus
Plantain family (Plantaginaceae)

Description: Rose-pink, bluish-purple, or dark purple flowers are arranged on one side of a smooth stem. The 2-lipped blossoms have 2 lobes above and 3 lobes below. Flowers are up to 2" long, and the 5th sterile stamen, or staminode, is densely covered with yellow hairs (the "beard" of the common name). The thick, hairless leaves may have a whitish coating, making them look pale. The entire leaves are 1–4" long and clasp the stem. Plants grow 4–20" tall.

Bloom Season: May to July

Habitat/Range: Frequently seen on grassy slopes and gravelly or wooded sites in the foothills and montane ecosystems from Wyoming to New Mexico.

Comments: Also called purple beardtongue. Similar to onesided penstemon (*P. unilateralis*) because both species have flowers on 1 side of the stem, but *P. unilateralis* has no hairs on the staminode and has narrower, greener leaves. Formerly in the Figwort family (Scrophulariaceae).

LORAINE YEATTS

CHRIS KASSAR

MANY-FLOWERED PHLOX
Phlox multiflora
Phlox family (Polemoniaceae)

Description: Low mats of vegetation bear numerous pink, light blue, or white blossoms. Each ½" wide flower has 5 broad petals united at the base to create a slender tube, 5 sepals, and a 3-lobed style. Narrow, opposite leaves are ¼–1¼" long with entire margins. The simple leaves have rough surfaces and are hairless except for tiny stiff prickles at the base. Branched stems have a woody base, grow in clumps, and reach ¾–4" tall.

Bloom Season: May to July

Habitat/Range: Common in grassy areas, pine forests, and on slopes in the foothills, montane, subalpine, and alpine ecosystems from Montana to New Mexico.

Comments: Also called Rocky Mountain phlox. Cushion phlox (*P. pulvinata*) has broader, shorter leaves with sticky hairs and grows mainly in alpine areas.

WATER SMARTWEED
Persicaria amphibia
Synonym: *Polygonum amphibium*
Buckwheat family (Polygonaceae)

Description: Tiny yet showy rose-colored to bright pink flowers are arranged in tight oblong clusters on a thick, naked stalk. Flower clusters grow ⅓–1½" long. Large, alternate, leathery, oval leaves grow 3–6" long. This truly amphibious plant can grow on land or in the water. On land, the erect stems and leaves are covered with dense hairs, while underwater the stems and leaves are hairless. Underwater leaves end in blunt tips; on land, leaves have pointed tips. Stems can grow to 4' long.

Bloom Season: June to August

Habitat/Range: Found floating in shallow water or rooted on the shorelines of ponds and lakes and the banks of rivers and streams in montane ecosystems from Canada to New Mexico.

Comments: This species grows on every continent except Australia. Native Americans living on the plains used these as a source of food and medicine.

CHRIS KASSAR

CHRIS KASSAR

SHOOTING STAR
Dodecatheon pulchellum ssp. *pulchellum*
Primrose family (Primulaceae)

Description: Shooting star is a fitting name for these unique bright rose-pink blossoms. Each flower has 4 or 5 petals, bent sharply backward, revealing a yellow center inscribed with a wiggly, reddish-purple line. The 5 stamens form a black, dartlike point. One or more ¾–1½" long flowers attach to each leafless stalk. Around the stalk is a cluster of basal leaves that are 1¼–12" long. The smooth, oblong leaves usually are entire but may be barely toothed. Plants grow 4–16" tall.

Bloom Season: April to August

Habitat/Range: Abundant along streamsides and in moist meadows in the foothills, montane, subalpine, and alpine ecosystems from Alaska to New Mexico.

Comments: The Thompson Indian name for this plant means "beautiful maiden." The Okanagan people called it "curlew's bill."

ALPINE PRIMROSE
Primula angustifolia
Primrose family (Primulaceae)

Description: These brilliant pink, 5-petaled flowers have yellow centers. The ⅓–¾" wide blossoms have a small notch at the tip of each petal. Rosettes of short, narrow, fleshy basal leaves grow in clumps. The thick entire leaves fold upward. Usually 1 fragrant flower blooms from a stalk under 4" tall.

Bloom Season: May to August

Habitat/Range: Common in open subalpine areas and rocky alpine tundra slopes in the mountains of Colorado and occasionally in the mountains of northern New Mexico.

Comments: Also called fairy primrose. Occasionally, a variation with white blossoms can be found amid a population of pink flowers.

AL SCHNEIDER, WWW.SWCOLORADOWILDFLOWERS.COM

PRAIRIE SMOKE

Geum triflorum var. *triflorum*
Synonym: *Erythrocoma triflora*
Rose family (Rosaceae)

Description: From 3–6 urn-shaped, rose-pink flowers dangle from a hairy reddish stalk. The obvious parts of the ½" long blossoms are the pink bracts and sepals, while the light yellow, green, or white flower petals are barely visible. The pinnately compound, parsley-like leaves are 4–8" long and primarily basal. The 9–19 hairy leaflets are cut into 3–5 toothed segments. After being pollinated, the blossoms turn upward, and a tuft of feathery-tailed seeds develops. Stems may grow 6–24" tall.

Bloom Season: March to July

Habitat/Range: Found in meadows, aspen forests, and on hillsides in the foothills, montane, and subalpine ecosystems from Canada to New Mexico.

Comments: Also called pink plumes, old man's whiskers, torch flower, or 3-flowered avens. Historically, the roots were boiled to make tea and used as eyewash. Fields filled with these plants in seed give a hazy or smoky appearance, hence their common name.

CHRIS KASSAR

PARRY PRIMROSE

Primula parryi
Primrose family (Primulaceae)

Description: Its beautiful magenta flowers tower over other alpine plants, making this a favorite of mountain climbers. The 5-petaled flowers are ⅝–1¼" across with yellow centers. Blossoms have a small notch at the tip of the petals. Usually, 3–15 flowers grow in a rounded cluster atop a stout, leafless stalk. The 2–12" long basal leaves are arranged in a rosette and stand upright. Thick, smooth, bright green leaves are oblong and about as tall as the flower stalk. Plants grow 3–16" tall.

Bloom Season: June to August

Habitat/Range: Wet meadows, near boulders, and along streamsides in the subalpine and alpine ecosystems from Montana to New Mexico.

Comments: Flowers and foliage may have a skunky odor that probably attracts pollinators. Primrose is likely derived from *primus* meaning "first," referring to the early flowering of some species.

CHRIS KASSAR

STEVE OLSON

WILD ROSE
Rosa woodsii
Rose family (Rosaceae)

Description: Fragrant, 5-petaled, pale to bright pink blossoms with many yellow stamens adorn this thorny shrub. The 1½–2½" wide flowers usually appear in clusters of 2 or more. The 5 sticky sepals dry out and stay attached to the edible red fruit, which is called a hip. Alternate, pinnately compound leaves have 5 or more toothed leaflets and stipules at the base of the leaf stalk. The woody, branched stems bear thorns that are wide at the base. The round, hard hips stay on the shrub into the wintertime. This plant grows 2–10' tall and forms loose or dense thickets.

Bloom Season: May to August

Habitat/Range: Commonly found in a variety of habitats including meadows, on slopes, along roads, near streams, and at the edges of woods in the foothills, montane, and subalpine ecosystems from Canada to New Mexico.

Comments: Also called Woods' rose after Joseph Woods, an architect, botanist, and rose scholar. Rose hips, extremely rich in vitamin C, make a delectable trail snack and often taste best after the first frost. Just be sure to remove the inner seeds and hairs because these can irritate the digestive tract. Roses hybridize, so species may be hard to tell apart.

DAVIS MOUNTAINS MOCK VERVAIN
Glandularia bipinnatifida var. *ciliata*
Synonym: *Glandularia wrightii*
Vervain family (Verbenaceae)

Description: Showy pink to purple flowers grow in clusters atop branched stems. The tubular, ¼–½" wide blossoms have 5 lobes that are notched at the tip. Below the flowers are bracts and sepals that are often sticky. Opposite, twice pinnately divided leaves are ¾–3". The stems may be erect, or the base may lie along the ground. They are usually hairy and grow 4–23" tall.

Bloom Season: May to September

Habitat/Range: Found in fields and along roads in the foothills ecosystem of Arizona, Colorado, New Mexico, Texas, and Kansas.

Comments: *Glandula* is Latin for "acorn," referring to the shape of its seed. Its common name comes from the Davis Mountains of Texas.

WHITE FLOWERS

This section includes flowers that are pre-dominantly white or cream colored. White flowers grade into pale pink, pale blue, and light yellow, so readers should check the yellow, pink, and blue and purple sections as well.

CHRIS KASSAR

RED ELDERBERRY
Sambucus racemosa
Synonym: *S. microbotrys*
Muskroot family (Adoxaceae)

Description: Small white flowers are arranged in pyramidal clusters. The opposite, pinnately compound leaves have 5–7 toothed leaflets. Warty bumps cover the twigs. The clusters of small red to blackish berries are usually dry and bitter when raw. The shrubs grow 3–10' tall.

Bloom Season: April to July

Habitat/Range: Common in moist meadows, open forests, on hillsides, and near streams and roadsides in the montane and subalpine ecosystems from Canada to Colorado.

Comments: *Sambucus* is a Greek word for a musical instrument; the hollow stems can be used as whistles. Raw berries are unpalatable but make scrumptious jelly, pie, and jam. Berries are also a favorite of bear, deer, and elk, which bite off the entire cluster. Formerly in the Honeysuckle family (Caprifoliaceae).

STEVE OLSON / INSET DENVER BOTANIC GARDENS

SQUASHBERRY
Viburnum edule
Muskroot family (Adoxaceae)

Description: Clusters of white blossoms adorn this bush. The 5-lobed flowers have 5 stamens and 5 sepals. Simple leaves are toothed and may have 3 lobes, giving them the appearance of maple leaves. The opposite leaves are 1½–4¾" long. Branches are smooth, with brown or grayish new growth. The edible, roundish red fruits have pits like a cherry. This shrub grows 2–6½' tall.

Bloom Season: May to July

Habitat/Range: Found in forests and near streams in the foothills, montane, and subalpine ecosystems from Canada to Colorado.

Comments: Also called high bush cranberry, bush cranberry, or arrowwood. Despite the berries' strong smell, which is often compared to dirty socks, they make a tasty snack when turned into jelly, juice, or wine. Formerly in the Honeysuckle family (Caprifoliaceae).

SCOTT F. SMITH

CHRIS KASSAR

SAND LILY

Leucocrinum montanum
Agave family (Agavaceae)

Description: Several star-shaped white blossoms sit among grasslike, basal leaves. The bases of 6 tepals are fused to form a tube 1–3" long. The stemless flowers are 1–1¼" wide with 6 stamens topped by yellow pollen. The folded, narrow basal leaves are 2–8" long. This delicate plant grows 2–4" tall.

Bloom Season: March to June

Habitat/Range: Found in fields and open forests in the foothills and montane ecosystems from Montana to New Mexico.

Comments: Also called star lily. *Leucocrinum* is Greek for "white lily." According to William A. Weber and Ronald C. Wittmann (in *Colorado Flora: Eastern Slope*), this plant has a unique method for seed dispersal. The plant's ovary is underground; it elongates when mature, putting the seeds just beneath the soil surface. The next year's flower buds push up the previous season's ovary, scattering the seeds. Formerly in the Lily family (Liliaceae).

YUCCA

Yucca glauca
Agave family (Agavaceae)

Description: A raceme of creamy- or greenish-white, bell-shaped nodding blossoms grows on a woody stalk. The 1¼–2" wide and long flowers have 6 thick, edible tepals, 6 stamens, and a green style. The long, narrow, pointed leaves look like light-green daggers. The evergreen leaves are usually 10–33" long. Green, podlike fruits dry and split open to reveal round black seeds stacked like coins. The flowering stalks grow 1–5' high.

Bloom Season: May to July

Habitat/Range: Found in dry fields and on sunny hillsides in the foothills ecosystem from Montana to New Mexico.

Comments: Also called Spanish bayonet or soap-weed. The blossoms open wide in the evening, and the small pronuba moth (*Tegeticula yuccasella*) pollinates them. The female moth pierces the ovary and lays an egg. She then collects a ball of yucca pollen and packs it into the stigma, ensuring pollination. The pod produces many seeds, so there are some left after the moth larva has eaten its fill. Native Americans ate the young pods, made soap from the roots, and derived cordage from the leaf fibers. Formerly in the Lily family (Liliaceae).

CHRIS KASSAR

SCOTT F. SMITH

GRAY'S ANGELICA
Angelica grayi
Parsley family (Apiaceae)

Description: Tiny blossoms have whitish to greenish-gray petals. The flowers are arranged in numerous round clusters (umbels) that make up a larger, globular cluster resembling a wheel. The compound, pinnate, ovate leaves are divided into leaflets, often in 3s at the bottom and 2s as you continue up the leaf. The stout stem can range in color from maroon to green to yellow and in size from 6–24", depending on habitat.

Bloom Season: June to August

Habitat/Range: Found in shady sites, in moist meadows, and along streams in the montane, subalpine, and alpine ecosystems of Wyoming, Colorado, and northern New Mexico.

Comments: *Angelica* comes from the Latin for "angelic," in reference to the medicinal properties of some species. The specific epithet honors Asa Gray, 1810–1888, the most important taxonomist of his day and the originator of the Harvard herbarium.

WATER HEMLOCK
Cicuta maculata
Synonym: *Cicuta douglasii*
Parsley family (Apiaceae)

Description: Clusters of small whitish to green flowers grow in rounded clusters (umbels) about 2–4" across. The compound, pinnate, lance-shaped leaves are divided into 3s and have prominent veins that end at the base of the teeth. The stout, hollow, leafy stem grows 1½–7' tall. The seedlike fruits are ribbed.

Bloom Season: June to September

Habitat/Range: Found in wet areas, marshes, swamps, and along ditches and streams of foothills, montane, and subalpine ecosystems from Canada to New Mexico.

Comments: This plant is highly poisionous, as is the closely related poison hemlock (*Conium maculatum*), which has fernlike leaves, purple-spotted stems, and grows 1½–10' tall. Even small amounts of the poison in hemlock—cicutoxin—act on the central nervous system, leading to convulsions and possibly death. This plant was originally named for David Douglas, a Scotsman who collected and described many Rocky Mountain plants in the 1880s and had many species, including the Douglas fir, named in his honor.

ERNIE MARX

LORAINE YEATTS

POISON HEMLOCK
Conium maculatum
Parsley family (Apiaceae)

Description: Clusters of small white flowers grow atop this tall, weedy plant. The twice compound, fernlike leaves are 6–12" long. The green branched stems have purple spots. The seedlike fruits are ribbed. The smooth stems of this biennial plant grow 1½–10' tall.

Bloom Season: June to August

Habitat/Range: This exotic weed thrives in moist disturbed sites of the foothills and montane eco-systems from Canada to New Mexico.

Comments: This nonnative plant was introduced from Europe and continues to thrive across North America, Eurasia, and Africa. Ancient Greeks used juice from this poisonous plant to kill Socrates. Another poisonous member of this family is water hemlock (*Cicuta maculata*), which lacks the spotted stem and finely divided leaves.

COW PARSNIP
Heracleum maximum
Synonyms: *H. sphondylium* ssp. *montanum,*
H. lanatum
Parsley family (Apiaceae)

Description: Everything about this plant is huge, except its tiny white flowers, which have petals under ¼" long. The sweet-smelling blossoms are arranged in flat-topped clusters (umbels) that may be up to 1' wide. The broad leaves can be several feet wide and look similar to maple leaves. They are palmately cleft or compound and typically have 3 toothed leaflets. Large sheaths encase the base of each stem leaf. The small fruits are flat and have 2 broad wings, while the seeds are large, colorful, and have a pungent, parsley-like smell. The hollow, hairy stem can be more than ¾" in diameter and reaches 2½–8' tall.

Bloom Season: May to August

Habitat/Range: Found in wet meadows, open forests, and near streams in the foothills, montane, and subalpine ecosystems from Alaska to Arizona.

Comments: Linnaeus named this genus after the mythical hero Hercules because people thought the plant had powerful medicinal properties. The Blackfeet and other American Indians collected the stalks in spring and peeled, roasted, and ate them. This species could be confused with water hemlocks (*Cicuta* ssp.), a related and poisonous group of plants.

CHRIS KASSAR

LOVEROOT
Ligusticum porteri
Parsley family (Apiaceae)

Description: Tiny white flowers grouped in small flat-topped clusters form larger round umbels that sit gracefully atop a stout stalk. Flower heads begin with green or rosy blossoms but then flower fully into bright white flowers up to 4" across. The finely dissected, fernlike leaves arch upward and range in length from 6–36". They are pinnately compound with ovate leaflets. The small fruit is winged. The reddish, 1½–6' stem is hollow and branched. This plant often grows in dense stands.

Bloom Season: June to August

Habitat/Range: Very common in meadows, wet areas, and aspen groves in the foothills, montane, and subalpine ecosystems from Wyoming to New Mexico.

Comments: Also called osha, wild parsnip, Porter's lovage, and wild celery. Various Native American groups have used the roots to ward off rattlesnakes, soothe sore throats, and cure various illnesses, especially respiratory infections like colds, coughs, pneumonia, and flu. Wild populations are declining because collectors continue to dig up the plant for its medicinal roots. Because conservationists are concerned about its long-term viability, it has been ranked as a rare plant in the United States and has also been classified as "vulnerable." A similar species, fernleaf lovage (*L. tenuifolium*), has narrow leaflets and a slender stem, and is usually under 20" tall.

CHRIS KASSAR

YARROW
Achillea millefolium
Synonym: A. lanulosa
Aster family (Asteraceae)

Description: Five tiny white, sometimes pinkish, ray flowers surround a central yellow disk. Blossoms grow in crowded, flat-topped clusters that range from ¾–4" across. Long, narrow, feathery, and finely dissected fernlike leaves grow alternately along a tough, fibrous stem. This fragrant plant grows 6–40".

Bloom Season: June to September

Habitat/Range: Very commonly found on hillsides, in dry or moist open areas, and disturbed sites in foothills, montane, and subalpine environments from Alaska to New Mexico.

Comments: Yarrow has many medicinal properties. Taken internally, yarrow tea treats colds and fevers. When applied externally, it relieves burns, sores, pimples, and, perhaps most notably, acts as a styptic—a substance that stops bleeding. Legend has it that Achilles, a hero in Greek mythology, applied yarrow to soldiers' wounds in the battle of Troy, thereby saving the lives of many. *Millefolium* means "a thousand leaves," referring to the many fine segments of the leaves. William Weber, renowned botanist and author of *Colorado Flora*, states that *A. lanulosa* and *A. millefolium* are very closely related but different species, whereas John Kartesz (the authority for plant names in this book) treats them as one species under the name of *A. millefolium*, with *A. lanulosa* as a synonym.

STEVE OLSON

STEVE OLSON

PEARLY EVERLASTING
Anaphalis margaritacea
Aster family (Asteraceae)

Description: This plant looks like an oversize, leafy pussytoes *(Antennaria)*. Tight clusters of ¼" wide flower heads have small yellow disk flowers surrounded by numerous white bracts. Ray flowers are lacking. The stems and undersides of the leaves have whitish, woolly hairs. Narrow 1–5" long leaves are alternate, entire, and stalkless. This perennial is 9–24" tall.

Bloom Season: July to September

Habitat/Range: Found in open coniferous forests and burned sites, on hillsides, and along roads in the foothills, montane, and subalpine ecosystems from Canada to New Mexico.

Comments: This plant has many medicinal uses. Native Americans smoked the leaves to help with throat and lung problems, while poultices relieved stiff joints, bruises, swellings, and sores. The common name refers to their durability in flower arrangements.

ROCKY MOUNTAIN PUSSYTOES
Antennaria parvifolia
Aster family (Asteraceae)

Description: Flower heads that look like the pads of a cat's paw give this plant its common name. Usually, 3–8 heads containing only disk flowers are ¼" to just under ½" tall. The papery bracts around the flower heads have white or pinkish tips and a darkened base, but lack an obvious dark spot. Grayish ¼–1" long leaves are primarily basal with woolly hairs. The entire leaves are rounded at the tip and narrow toward the base. The vegetation spreads by leafy runners to form mats. Stems are 2–6" tall.

Bloom Season: June to September

Habitat/Range: Common in dry meadows and open woods of the foothills, montane, and subalpine ecosystems from Canada to New Mexico.

Comments: Also called sunloving catspaw and mountain, Nuttall's, or small-leaved pussytoes. May be confused with the taller, leafy-stemmed pearly everlasting (*Anaphalis margaritacea*), but *A. parvifolia* has relatively large basal leaves and smaller, or no, upper stem leaves.

89

© Al Schneider

NATIONAL PARK SERVICE

COLORADO THISTLE
Cirsium scariosum var. *coloradense*
Synonym: *C. coloradense*
Aster family (Asteraceae)

Description: White to purplish disk flowers are arranged in heads that are ¾–2" wide and 1–1¾" tall. There typically are 1–8 heads per stem. The hairy bracts have spiny tips while the upper surfaces of the leaves lack spines. The simple, alternate leaves are lobed, lanceolate, and green above with undersides of silver. This perennial may be stemless or have stout stems up to 4' high.

Bloom Season: June to September

Habitat/Range: Found in moist meadows and aspen forests, on hillsides, and near streams in the foothills, montane, and subalpine ecosystems. Common in the mountains of Colorado,

with outlying populations found in northern New Mexico and southeastern Wyoming.

Comments: Also called elk thistle. The peeled stems and roots are edible. The genus name comes from *cirsos*, which means "swollen vein" in Greek, referring to the belief that thistle was a remedy for clogged veins. Wavy-leaved thistle (*C. undulatum*) is native to the Rockies and fairly common on dry, open sites from plains to montane zones. It has large, showy, pink to purple flower heads, smooth leaves and stalks, and dense woolly hairs covering its plants.

NATIONAL PARK SERVICE

AL SCHNEIDER, WWW.SWCOLORADOWILDFLOWERS.COM

CUTLEAF DAISY
Erigeron compositus
Aster family (Asteraceae)

Description: This species usually has white, pink, or blue ray flowers and yellow disk flowers, but sometimes it lacks rays. The heads are ½–1" wide, and phyllaries are often hairy and tipped with purple. Leaves are mainly basal, usually hairy and fan-shaped, and divided 1–4 times into narrow 3-lobed segments. Several stems grow in clumps with each stem carrying a single blossom. This perennial grows 2–10" high.

Bloom Season: June to August

Habitat/Range: Found in open pine forests, dry meadows, scree slopes, boulder fields, and gravelly areas in the foothills, montane, subalpine, and alpine ecosystems from Alaska to Arizona.

Comments: Also called dwarf mountain fleabane or gold buttons (if it lacks ray flowers). People once believed if fleabane was burned, it would drive fleas and other insects away. As cattle overgraze an area, the numbers of this plant increase. This species may be confused with *E. flagellaris*, but the habitat and sage-green leaves of *E. compositus*, which are divided multiple times, make it easier to differentiate.

WHIPLASH DAISY
Erigeron flagellaris
Aster family (Asteraceae)

Description: From 50–100 white ray flowers surround a circle of densely packed, bright yellow disk flowers. The undersides of the rays are pinkish, lavender, or bluish. Buds are pink and nodding. One ¾" wide blossom sits atop each stem. The phyllaries under the flowers have sticky hairs. The mainly basal, hairy leaves are narrow, entire, and up to 1½" long. This plant grows 2–16" tall. Runners extend on the surface, colonizing large areas and taking root to form new plants.

Bloom Season: March to August

Habitat/Range: Common in meadows and on grassy hillsides in the foothills, montane, and subalpine ecosystems from Canada to New Mexico.

Comments: Also called trailing or running fleabane. The specific name *flagellaris* means "whiplike," referring to the runners.

NATIONAL PARK SERVICE

BARRY BRECKLING

BLACKHEAD DAISY

Erigeron melanocephalus
Aster family (Asteraceae)

Description: Typically, 50–70 white or pinkish ray flowers surround a central yellow disk, and 1 solitary head, measuring 1–1½" across, sits atop each stem. The green bracts have woolly, black, or dark purple hairs. Basal leaves are spoon shaped and up to 1½" long. This species typically has a few small leaves high on the flower stalk. The hairy stems of this perennial grow 2–6" tall.

Bloom Season: July to August

Habitat/Range: Common in moist meadows, including those surrounding melting snowbanks, and on hillsides in the subalpine and alpine ecosystems of Wyoming, Utah, Colorado, and New Mexico.

Comments: Aven Nelson, an accomplished botanist and professor at the Univeristy of Wyoming, first collected *E.melanocephalus* in the Medicine Bow Mountains of Wyoming. *Melanocephalus* is Greek for "black head." In alpine areas, this plant may be confused with the usually bluish- or lavender-flowered alpine fleabane (*E. grandiflorus*), which has bracts with lighter-colored white or red woolly hairs.

WHITE PRAIRIE ASTER

Symphyotrichum falcatum
Synonyms: *Virgulus falcatus, Aster falcatus*
Aster Family (Asteraceae)

Description: Subshrub with 1–5+ moderately to densely hairy stems containing 1–10+ heads per branch. Heads are ½" high and wide and have 15–35 white rays surrounding 8–30 yellow disk corollas that become brown over time. Light grayish-green leaves are firm with entire margins and blades that are broadest above the middle. This plant forms large patches and spreads by underground runners.

Bloom Season: July to September

Habitat/Range: Found in foothills, woodland openings, fields, roadsides, and dry montane meadows from Canada to New Mexico.

Comments: Zuni Indians mixed ground blossoms of *S. falcatum* with yucca suds to create a strengthening wash for newborns. Navajo Indians made a lotion and used it as a snake bite remedy**.**

CHRISTINA MACLEOD

AL SCHNEIDER, WWW.SWCOLORADOWILDFLOWERS.COM

STEMLESS EASTER DAISY

Townsendia exscapa
Aster family (Asteraceae)

Description: White or pinkish ray flowers and yellow disk flowers make up a head about 1" wide. Stemless flowers are clustered directly atop the basal leaves. The bracts are lance shaped and lacking a tuft of hair at the tip. Narrow, simple ¼–2" long grayish leaves grow in dense clusters. This perennial is only 1–2" tall.

Bloom Season: March to June

Habitat/Range: Dry fields, hillsides, and pinyon-juniper woodlands in the foothills and montane ecosystems from Canada to New Mexico.

Comments: This is one of the earliest blooming flowers of the foothills and is the most widely distributed of the *Townsendia* genus within the Southern Rockies. The genus name honors David Townsend (1787–1858), a bank clerk and accomplished amateur botanist who collected over 700 species of plants from near where he lived in Pennsylvania.

FENDLER'S WATERLEAF

Hydrophyllum fendleri
Borage family (Boraginaceae)

Description: Loose, branched clusters of cream to lavender flowers sit on long stalks atop a hairy stem. Each ¼–⅜" wide blossom has 5 rounded lobes and 5 white to light purple projecting stamens. Sepals are covered with bristly hairs. The 2¼–12" long leaves are simple, alternate, and pinnately divided into 5–13 segments with toothed edges. Stems have hairs that point downward. This plant grows 8–36" tall.

Bloom Season: April to August

Habitat/Range: Found in moist, shady sites and open areas in the foothills and montane ecosystems from Wyoming to New Mexico.

Comments: This species is named for August Fendler, a collector in the mid-19th century who did the majority of his collecting in 1846 when he accompanied US troops from Bent's Fort to Santa Fe, New Mexico, during the Mexican-American War. Fendler collected this plant in 1846–1847 in the mountains above Santa Fe. The similar, but shorter, ball-head waterleaf (*H. capitatum*) has blue or lavender flowers in tight, round clusters. Formerly in the Waterleaf family (Hydrophyllaceae).

CHRIS KASSAR

CHRIS KASSAR

MINER'S CANDLE

Oreocarya virgata
Synonym: *Cryptantha virgata*
Borage family (Boraginaceae)

Description: Small white flowers with 5 lobes look like forget-me-nots, which also are members of the Borage family. Numerous blossoms, together with long, leafy bracts spread along a tall, stout hairy stem. The narrow, 1–4" long leaves are covered with stiff hairs and grow perpendicular to the flower stalk. A single 8–24" spikelike stem is typically unbranched.

Bloom Season: May to August

Habitat/Range: Found in dry fields and on slopes in the foothills and montane ecosystems of Wyoming and Colorado.

Comments: The generic name *Oreocarya* means "mountain nut," referring to the nutlike seeds. Its specific name, *virgata,* means "wand-like."

HEARTLEAF BITTERCRESS

Cardamine cordifolia
Mustard family (Brassicaceae)

Description: Bright white 4-petaled flowers ½–¾" long are arranged in a rounded cluster on a leafy stem. Like other mustards, the 4 petals of each blossom form a cross shape. The simple, heart-shaped leaves are ¾–2" in length, long stalked, and have wavy edges. Slightly flattened seedpods are ¾–1½" long. This perennial grows 4–30" tall in clumps.

Bloom Season: May to August

Habitat/Range: Found in moist meadows, wet forests, and near streams and springs in the montane and subalpine ecosystems from Montana to New Mexico.

Comments: Also called brook cress. The specific epithet is derived from the Latin word *cord* meaning "heart" and *folia* meaning "leaf."

NATIONAL PARK SERVICE

NATIONAL PARK SERVICE

WILD CANDYTUFT

Noccaea fendleri ssp. *glauca*
Synonyms: *N. montana, Thlaspi montanum*
Mustard family (Brassicaceae)

Description: Small white to lavender flowers appear in clusters atop smooth stems. The four petals are ¼" long and arranged in a cross shape with green to purple sepals below each petal. Smooth, alternate leaves clasp the stem. Ovate or spoon-shaped basal leaves are ½–2" long and may be toothed. Flat, heart-shaped seedpods have pointed tips that grow less than ½" long. This perennial has one or more unbranched stems that grow 1–16" tall.

Bloom Season: April to August

Habitat/Range: Common in forests and on hillsides in the foothills, montane, subalpine, and alpine ecosystems from Montana to New Mexico.

Comments: Also called Fendler's pennycress, this is one of the earliest flowering plants in the foothills.

MOUSE-EAR CHICKWEED

Cerastium arvense ssp. *strictum*
Synonym: *C. strictum*
Pink family (Caryophyllaceae)

Description: Open clusters of white, ⅜–½" flowers grow atop thin, straight stems. The flower has 5 petals, each with a deep notch in the tip, and the petals are at least twice as long as the 5 separate sepals. Bracts under the flower cluster have thin, dry edges. The weak stem holds a few narrow, opposite, and deeply veined leaves that measure ⅜–1½" long and are covered with velvety hairs. The fruit is a cylindrical, seed-bearing capsule. This erect perennial often grows in clumps. The 2–12" stems may be sticky.

Bloom Season: April to August

Habitat/Range: Commonly found in dry meadows, open pine forests, and on rocky slopes in the foothills, montane, subalpine, and alpine ecosystems from Canada to New Mexico.

Comments: Also known as prairie mouse-ear chickweed or field chickweed. Botanist William Weber places this species in the Chickweed family (Alsinaceae). Mountain chickweed (*C. beeringianum*), which grows in alpine ecosystems, has fewer flowers, sepals that are almost as long as the petals, and broader leaves.

NATIONAL PARK SERVICE

LORAINE YEATTS

ALPINE SANDWORT
Minuartia obtusiloba
Synonyms: *Lidia obtusiloba, Areneria obtusiloba*
Pink family (Caryophyllaceae)

Description: Numerous tiny white flowers sit atop stems that barely reach beyond a mat of miniscule mosslike leaves. Blossoms are only ⅜" wide, with 10 stamens, 3 styles, and 5 rounded petals that are longer than the green, inwardly curved, blunt-tipped sepals. The mainly basal leaves are less than ¼" long. Clustered stems have woody bases and very short, sticky hairs. This mat-forming plant grows ⅜–2⅜" tall.

Bloom Season: June to September

Habitat/Range: Very common in sandy, windy, or rocky alpine areas from Alaska to New Mexico.

Comments: William Weber, botanist and author of *Colorado Flora*, places sandworts in the Chickweed family (Alsinaceae).

SINGLE DELIGHT
Moneses uniflora
Synonym: *Pyrola uniflora*
Heath family (Ericaceae)

Description: One nodding, fragrant white flower grows atop a leafless stem. Each waxy blossom is ¾–1" across and usually has 5 petals, 10 stamens, and a straight style topped by a 5-parted stigma. Roundish, evergreen basal leaves have rounded teeth and grow ½–1" long. This smooth plant may grow 2–5" tall. Commonly found within a few feet of other individuals because it often reproduces from its underground roots.

Bloom Season: June to August

Habitat/Range: Found in moist, shady coniferous forests and near streams in the montane and sub-alpine ecosystems from Alaska to New Mexico.

Comments: Also called one-flowered winter-green, star pyrola, wood nymph, or waxflower. *Moneses* comes from the Greek *monos* ("one") and *hesis* ("delight"). Formerly in the Wintergreen family (Pyrolaceae).

MARY DUBLER

CHRIS KASSAR

ROCKY MOUNTAIN LOCO
Oxytropis sericea
Bean family (Fabaceae)

Description: White or cream-colored flowers usually have a purple spot on the pointy-tipped keel. The pealike, ¾–1" long blossoms grow in clusters atop a leafless stalk. Leaves are basal, 2–12" long, and covered with grayish hairs. The pinnately compound leaves have 11–21 lanceolate leaflets. The leathery pods are up to 1" long. The plants usually grow 6–16" tall in clumps.

Bloom Season: April to September

Habitat/Range: Found in fields, meadows, and on hillsides in the foothills, montane, and subalpine ecosystems from Canada to New Mexico.

Comments: Also called white, silverleaf, or silky loco. Pink flowers may indicate a hybrid with Lambert's loco (*O. lambertii*).

ARCTIC GENTIAN
Gentiana algida
Synonym: *Gentianodes algida*
Gentian family (Gentianaceae)

Description: These creamy-white to yellow-green goblet-shaped flowers are some of the last bloomers to grace the alpine tundra. The 1–1¾" tall blossoms have 4 or 5 pointed lobes marked with blue to purple lines, spots, and/or blotches. There are 1–3 flowers atop each stem. Narrow entire leaves are 2–5" long. Some of the opposite, stalkless leaves clasp the stem. This perennial grows 2–8" tall.

Bloom Season: July to September

Habitat/Range: Found in meadows and near streams in the subalpine and alpine ecosystems from Montana to New Mexico.

Comments: Gentians also grow in Europe, Asia, and New Guinea. The specific epithet, *algida*, is from the Latin for "cold."

97

NATIONAL PARK SERVICE BY RUSSELL SMITH

LORAINE YEATTS

RICHARDSON'S GERANIUM
Geranium richardsonii
Geranium family (Geraniaceae)

Description: Dark pink or purple veins stand out against 5 white or pinkish petals. The 1" wide blossoms have 10 stamens, and the flower clusters have purple-tipped soft hairs on the lower sides. Sticky hairs cover the typically paired flower stalks. The long-stalked leaves are palmately lobed into 3–7 segments. This perennial often has just 1 stem, which is 1–3' high. The pointy fruit is 1" long.

Bloom Season: May to September

Habitat/Range: Found in moist, shady meadows, in aspen groves, and near streams in the foothills, montane, and subalpine ecosystems from Canada to New Mexico.

Comments: Also called white geranium or cranesbill. The common and specific names honor the 19th-century arctic explorer Dr. John Richardson. May be confused with Fremont's geranium (*G. caespitosum*), which has many flowering stems, grows in a drier, bushier habitat, and is common in the foothills. Although often described as having pink flowers, *G. caespitosum* is often white, so it is better to differentiate using habitat and growth patterns.

CLIFF FENDLER BUSH
Fendlera rupicola
Synonym: *Fendlera falcata*
Hydrangea Family (Hydrangeaceae)

Description: Numerous large, fragrant, white or pink-tinged flowers cover this multibranched shrub. The 4 flower petals are as long as ¾" and have a narrow stalked base. Each flower has 8 stamens with broad, petal-like filaments that fork into 2 lobes near the anthers. Leaves are simple, lanceolate, and thick with rolled margins. Stem bark begins as a lustrous reddish tan, becoming darker with age. These showy shrubs grow 3–6' tall.

Bloom Season: May to July

Habitat/Range: Found on rocky hillsides in oak and pine woodlands of the foothills and montane ecosystems in Colorado, Utah, and New Mexico.

Comments: Also called false mock orange. This species can sometimes be mistaken for mock oranges (*Philadelphus* spp.), which are distinguished by having numerous stamens with round filaments. In Latin, *rupicola* means "rock dweller," referring to *F. rupicola*'s preferred habitat.

CHRIS KASSAR

MARIPOSA LILY
Calochortus gunnisonii
Lily family (Liliaceae)

Description: These beautiful and delicate cup-shaped flowers have 3 broad whitish, pinkish, or pale lavender petals, 3 narrow light green sepals, and a 3-parted stigma. Each petal has a broad strip of yellow hairs above the gland at its base. Blossoms grow up to 2" across and are characterized by a broad purple band encircling the center of the flower. Each stem usually has 1 to several flowers. The grasslike alternate and basal leaves are entire and have parallel veins. Unbranched stems are 10–20" tall.

Bloom Season: April to August

Habitat/Range: Found in meadows, open forests, and on hillsides in the foothills, montane, and subalpine ecosystems from Montana to New Mexico.

Comments: Also called sego lily. Members of the Ute tribe taught Mormon settlers in Utah about the plant's edible, rootlike corm. Captain J. W. Gunnison, for whom this flower is named, was an explorer and the trip leader for the fatal Gunnison expedition. After finishing a survey for the railroad, a band of Utes attacked and killed Gunnison and 7 of his companions; 1 of these men, a botanist named Frederick Creutzfeldt, collected the first sample of this plant months earlier. Some botanists place this in the Mariposa family (Calochortaceae).

LORAINE YEATTS

CHRIS KASSAR

ALPLILY
Lloydia serotina
Lily family (Liliaceae)

Description: Dainty, white, funnel-shaped blossoms have 6 separate, oblong tepals that are yellow at the base, purplish on the outside, and have pale green or purple veins. Usually there is 1 erect or nodding flower per stem. The blossoms are about ¾" wide and have 6 white-tipped stamens. The basal leaves are 2–8" long and very slender. Alternate stem leaves are much smaller. The fruit is a 3-parted capsule. The slender stems grow 2–6" tall.

Bloom Season: June to July

Habitat/Range: Found in rocky crevices, meadows, and on ridges in the upper subalpine and alpine ecosystems from Alaska to New Mexico.

Comments: Also called alpine lily. The generic name honors Welsh botanist Edward Lloyd, who discovered this plant in the mountains of Wales in the late 17th century.

TWISTED STALK
Streptopus amplexifolius
Synonym: *S. fassettii*
Lily family (Liliaceae)

Description: Greenish-white to cream-colored, almost spider-shaped flowers dangle from kinked stalks, located where the leaves attach to the stem. The blossoms are about ⅜" long with 6 tepals that curve backward. Alternate, stalkless leaves clasp the stem. The ovate 3–4" long leaves have parallel veins. The oblong or oval berries are orange-red and smooth. The stems are arched, branched, and lack hairs. This plant grows 1–3½' tall.

Bloom Season: May to August

Habitat/Range: Found in moist forests and near streams in the foothills, montane, and subalpine ecosystems from Alaska to New Mexico.

Comments: *Streptopus* means "twisted foot," referring to the bent flower stalks. *Amplexor* means "to surround" in Latin, and *folius* means "leaf," referring to the way the base of each leaf clasps the stem. Botanist William Weber places this genus in the Bellwort family (Uvulariaceae).

CHRIS KASSAR

DEATH CAMAS
Anticlea elegans
Synonym: *Zigadenus elegans*
False Hellebore family (Melanthiaceae)

Description: As its common name implies, this elegant flower is poisonous. The ½–¾" wide, star-shaped blossoms are borne in racemes near the top of the stem. Each flower has 6 creamy white tepals with notched projections at each tip, yellowish-green glands at each base, and 6 stamens. The smooth 6–12" long leaves look like wide blades of grass and may be slightly folded. Leaves appear mainly at the base of the stems. The unbranched stems grow 6–27" tall.

Bloom Season: June to August

Habitat/Range: Found in grassy meadows, forests, and near streams in the foothills, montane, subalpine, and alpine ecosystems from Alaska to New Mexico.

Comments: Also called wand lily. All parts of this plant contain the alkaloid zygadenine, a toxin said to be more potent than strychnine. Poisonings occur because people confuse these bulbs with those of edibles like wild onion, mariposas, or fritillaries. Formerly in the Lily family (Liliaceae).

ALPINE SPRING BEAUTY
Claytonia megarhiza
Synonym: *C. arctica megarhiza*
Candy-Flower family (Montiaceae)

Description: Flowers with 5 white or pink petals and reddish veins grow in round patches amid a tight rosette of fleshy, basal leaves. The ¾" wide blossoms have 2 sepals and 5 stamens. The 1–8" long simple leaves are thick and smooth. The spoon-shaped leaves begin red but become green as they gain chlorophyll with age. This low plant only grows to 5" tall.

Bloom Season: May to August

Habitat/Range: Found on gravelly slopes and in rocky areas of the alpine tundra from Montana to New Mexico.

Comments: Also called big-rooted spring beauty because of its thick, long taproot. The root and succulent leaves help the plant collect and retain water in the tundra's drying winds. This species could be confused with spring beauty (*C. lanceolata*), but *C. megarhiza*'s spoon-shaped leaves, dense basal cluster, and preference for rocky sites help with differentiation. Formerly in the Purslane family (Portulacaceae).

STEMLESS EVENING PRIMROSE
Oenothera caespitosa ssp. *macroglottis*
Evening Primrose family (Onagraceae)

Description: These huge white flowers are low to the ground. The showy blossoms are 2–4" across and fragrant. The 4 heart-shaped petals have slight indentations in the tip, and the 4 hairy sepals are bent down. The 4-parted stigma is obvious, and there are 8 stamens. The flowers are stemless but have a 2–4" long floral tube (a hypanthium) that may be mistaken for a stem. Fleshy, lance-shaped basal leaves are 1–6" long and have wavy or toothed margins.

Bloom Season: May to August

Habitat/Range: Found on gravelly hillsides and along roads and trails in the foothills, montane, and subalpine ecosystems from Canada to New Mexico.

Comments: Sometimes called tufted evening primrose or moon rose. The flowers usually bloom in the late afternoon or evening, only to wither from the heat and sun by the following afternoon, at which point the blossoms turn pink and close. *Caespitosa* means "tufted," in reference to the dense clumps of basal leaves and stems.

AL SCHNEIDER, WWW.SWCOLORADOWILDFLOWERS.COM

STEVE OLSON

CUTLEAF EVENING PRIMROSE
Oenothera coronopifolia
Evening Primrose family (Onagraceae)

Description: These flowers look like a smaller version of the blossoms of the stemless evening primrose (*Oenothera caespitosa* ssp. *macroglottis*). Like its relative, the cutleaf evening primrose has 4 petals, a 4-parted stigma, and 8 stamens. The white, ½–1¼" wide flowers appear where the upper leaves meet the stem. The large blossoms turn a pinkish color as they age. Short, deeply cut stem leaves are toothed or pinnately divided into narrow lobes. This perennial often grows in colonies, and each hairy, branched, or simple stem is 2–12" tall.

Bloom Season: May to August

Habitat/Range: Found in meadows and along roads in the foothills and montane ecosystems from Wyoming to New Mexico.

Comments: Sphinx moths (Sphingidae family) pollinate many flowers in this genus. The white blossoms stand out at night, making it easier for pollinators to find them. Members of the Evening Primrose family (Onagraceae) are unrelated to true primroses (Primulaceae). They share a similar name thanks to a botanist who was describing a new eastern United States species of *Oenothera* in the 1600s. Its fragrant smell reminded him of Europe's wild primroses, so he labeled them as such.

RATTLESNAKE PLANTAIN ORCHID
Goodyera oblongifolia
Orchid family (Orchidaceae)

Description: Rattlesnake plantain is known more for its striking leaves than for its inconspicuous blossoms. The greenish-white flowers are ¼–⅜" long and arranged in a loosely spiraled spike. Dark green, leathery leaves are typically mottled with dark green or striped white along the midrib and veins. The simple basal leaves are 2–4" long with pointy tips. Soft, short hairs cover the stem, which grows 4–16" tall.

Bloom Season: July to September

Habitat/Range: Found in forests in the foothills, montane, and subalpine ecosystems from Alaska to New Mexico.

Comments: The generic name honors John Goodyer, a 17th-century English naturalist. The common name refers to the leaves, which bear markings that look like a rattlesnake's skin. A similar species, *G. repens*, is smaller, has shorter leaves that are 1–1¼" long and is rare in Colorado, but more common in New Mexico.

103

SCOTT F. SMITH

SCOTT F. SMITH

WHITE BOG ORCHID

Piperia dilatata var. *albiflora*
Synonyms: *Limnorchis dilatata* ssp. *albiflora,*
Habenaria dilatata
Orchid family (Orchidaceae)

Description: Small, fragrant, white flowers and light green bracts are clustered atop a leafy stem. The blossom's hood is made up of 1 sepal and 2 petals. Another 2 sepals spread outward to the sides like wings. The lower petal is a tonguelike lip with a spur in the back. Alternate, lance-shaped leaves clasp the stem. Most of the 1½–8" long leaves appear at the base of a 4–24" unbranched stem.

Bloom Season: June to September

Habitat/Range: Found in bogs, near streamsides, and in other wet areas of the montane, subalpine, and alpine ecosystems from Alaska to New Mexico.

Comments: Also called scentbottle, bog rein orchid, or bog candle. Compare this flower to the similar-looking hooded lady's tresses (*Spiranthes romanzoffiana*), which lacks a spur and has flowers arranged in a tight spiral.

HOODED LADY'S TRESSES

Spiranthes romanzoffiana
Orchid family (Orchidaceae)

Description: Numerous white flowers arranged in 1–4 vertical rows gently spiral up to the top of the stem to create a flower spike about 4' long. These ¼–½" long blossoms lack a spur. Two petals and 3 sepals create a hood over a smaller lower lip petal. The bottom lip bends downward and has a jagged, toothed tip. The alternate, mainly basal leaves are lance shaped, vertical, and 2–10" long. These perennial plants grow 6–16" tall.

Bloom Season: June to September

Habitat/Range: Found in moist meadows, open woods, and along streamsides in the foothills, montane, and subalpine ecosystems from Alaska to New Mexico.

Comments: The generic name *Spiranthes* means "spiral flower." Compare to white bog orchid (*Piperia dilatata* var. *albiflora*), which looks similar but has a spur protruding out the back and flowers arranged in a cluster, not a spiral.

NATIONAL PARK SERVICE

LORAINE YEATTS

PARRY'S LOUSEWORT

Pedicularis parryi
Broomrape family (Orobanchaceae)

Description: A cluster of creamy white, yellow-ish, or pinkish beaked flowers adorns the top of smooth stems. The hooded upper lip of the flower has a short straight beak at its tip and looks some-what like the head of a goose. The blossoms are ½–1" long and interspersed with green bracts. The mainly basal, fernlike leaves are deeply pinnately divided and 2–4¾" long. Stem leaves are smaller. This plant often grows in clusters 4–16" tall.

Bloom Season: June to August

Habitat/Range: Common in meadows and on grav-elly slopes in the subalpine and alpine ecosystems from Montana to New Mexico.

Comments: Also called alpine lousewort. This plant may be confused with Canada lousewort (*P. canadensis*), whose leaves are not as deeply divided. Canada lousewort is usually found in the foothills and montane ecosystems. Also, compare to parrrot's beak (*P. racemosa*), which has white flowers with a broad, 3-lobed lower lip, sickle-shaped upper lip, and downward-curving beak. Formerly in the Figwort family (Scrophulariaceae).

SNOWLOVER

Chionophila jamesii
Plantain family (Plantaginaceae)

Description: Cream-colored or greenish-white tubular flowers are clustered on 1 side of the stem. The ⅜–¾" long blossoms are double lipped, with 2 lobes above and 3 below. The flowers have 5 stamens, and the 5th one is sterile. Leaves are mainly basal, spoon shaped, fleshy, and entire. Stem leaves are smaller and narrower. This peren-nial grows 2–4" tall.

Bloom Season: June to August

Habitat/Range: Found in moist, gravelly areas and near melting snowbanks on the alpine tundra of Wyoming, Colorado, and New Mexico.

Comments: In Greek, *Chionophila* means "snow lover." The specific epithet honors Edwin James, the botanist who collected specimens of this plant on a climb up Pikes Peak in 1820. Formerly in the Figwort family (Scrophulariaceae).

SCOTT F. SMITH / INSET NATIONAL PARK SERVICE BY RUSSELL SMITH

AMERICAN BISTORT
Bistorta bistortoides
Synonym: *Polygonum bistortoides*
Buckwheat family (Polygonaceae)

Description: Tiny white or pinkish flowers are arranged in a tight, oblong cluster (raceme) atop a tall, slender stem. The broad, funnel-shaped blossoms have 5 sepals and protruding stamens. The flower heads are 1–2" long and less than ¾" wide. The mainly basal leaves are stalked and 4–10" long. The stem leaves are narrow, smaller, and unstalked. The unbranched stem grows 8–27" tall.

Bloom Season: June to September

Habitat/Range: Common in moist meadows and near streams in the montane, subalpine, and alpine ecosystems from Canada to New Mexico.

Comments: Also called western bistort or miner's socks because of its unpleasant odor. The roots are edible and best if roasted. The similar-looking snowball saxifrage (*Micranthes rhomboidea*) typically has flowers in a round cluster and fleshy basal leaves.

CHRIS KASSAR

ALPINE BISTORT
Bistorta vivipara
Synonym: *Polygonum viviparum*
Buckwheat family (Polygonaceae)

Description: This smaller relative of American bistort (*B.bistortoides*) has a slender flower cluster that is less than ½" wide and 1–4" long. Below the white or pinkish flowers are small, dark bulblets that fall off and grow into new plants. Stalked basal leaves are ¾–3½" long. The alternate, stalkless stem leaves, smaller and narrower than the lower leaves, may clasp the stem and often have edges that roll downward. This unbranched plant often grows in scattered colonies, and each plant reaches 4–12" tall.

Bloom Season: June to September

Habitat/Range: Found in grassy open areas, tundra, moist meadows, and near streams in the subalpine and alpine ecosystems from Alaska to New Mexico.

Comments: In Latin, *vivus* means "alive," and *parere* means "to bring forth." Thus, the species name, *vivipara* refers to the fact that a viviparous plant asexually produces plants genetically identical to itself. In the case of *B.vivipara*, bulblets are produced below the tiny flowers, drop off, and create new plants.

STEVE OLSON/INSET SCOTT F. SMITH

BANEBERRY
Actaea rubra ssp. *arguta*
Buttercup family (Ranunculaceae)

Description: Numerous tiny white flowers form rounded clusters atop a slender stalk. Flowers have many 5–10 slender petals, 3–5 sepals, and many stamens that give the blossom a feathery appearance. The few large leaves are pinnately compound and typically divided into 3s. Leaflets are sharp toothed. Flowers soon drop off, giving way to shiny red, or occassionally white, berries that are about ¼" long and poisonous. This branched perennial usually grows 1–3' tall.

Bloom Season: May to July

Habitat/Range: Found in moist, shady forests and along streams in the foothills, montane, and subalpine ecosystems from Alaska to New Mexico.

Comments: Also called snakeberry or chinaberry. *Bane* is derived from a German word for "death," an appropriate name since the berries contain cardiogenic toxins that can cause cardiac arrest once in the bloodstream. Native Americans used the berry's juice to make poisonous arrow tips and the root to create conconctions that would treat arthritis, syphilis, pain, and colds and coughs. William Weber places baneberry in the Hellebore family (Helleboraceae).

CHRIS KASSAR

CHRIS KASSAR

NARCISSUS ANEMONE
Anemone narcissiflora var. *zephyra*
Synonym: *Anemonastrum narcissiflorum* ssp. *zephyrum*
Buttercup family (Ranunculaceae)

Description: From 1–4 flowers usually sit atop each stout stem. There are 4–20 cream-colored or yellowish petal-like sepals and numerous stamens. The sepals are ⅜–⅝" long. The leaves are mainly basal and palmately divided into deep, narrow lobes. Whorled or opposite stem leaves are stalkless. The stems of this 4–16" perennial have long hairs.

Bloom Season: June to August

Habitat/Range: Found in moist meadows of the subalpine and alpine ecosystems in Colorado and Wyoming.

Comments: Also called alpine anemone.

MARSH MARIGOLD
Caltha leptosepala
Synonym: *Psychrophila leptosepala*
Buttercup family (Ranunculaceae)

Description: A single blossom grows atop each thick, leafless stem. The upper surfaces of the 5–15 oblong sepals are white, and the bottom surfaces are bluish. The flowers, which lack petals, are typically 1–2" across and have numerous yellow stamens. The thick, waxy, oblong basal leaves are smooth and 3–8" long. The edges are entire or wavy. This plant grows 1–8" tall, often in clumps.

Bloom Season: June to August

Habitat/Range: Commonly found in wet sites, especially near melting snowbanks, in the subalpine and alpine ecosystems from Canada to New Mexico.

Comments: Also called elk's lip, referring to the long leaf's shape. *Caltha* is Latin for "marigold," and *lepto* is Greek for "fine." The synonym *psychrophilia* means "cold lover," referring to the fact that these often grow at the edge of receding snowbanks. Botanist William A. Weber places marsh marigold in the Hellebore family (Helleboraceae).

CHRIS KASSAR

STEVE OLSON

GLOBEFLOWER
Trollius laxus ssp. *albiflorus*
Synonym: *T. albiflorus*
Buttercup family (Ranunculaceae)

Description: The blossom of this plant has 5–9 cream-colored or whitish petal-like sepals that are oval shaped. Usually 1 flower sits atop each leafy stem. The 1–1½" wide blossoms have 15–25 inconspicuous yellow petals that surround numerous stamens. Alternate and basal leaves are palmately dissected, deeply cut, and toothed. The smooth stems of this perennial grow 4–23" tall in groups.

Bloom Season: April to August

Habitat/Range: Found in wet or moist sites in the montane, subalpine, and alpine ecosystems from Canada to Colorado.

Comments: Often found with the similar-looking marsh marigold *(Caltha leptosepala)*, which has broader, unlobed leaves, 8–10 narrower white sepals streaked with blue on their backs, and lacks the tiny yellow petals that illuminate the center of each globeflower. William Weber, botanist, places globeflower in the Hellebore family (Helleboraceae).

FENDLER'S CEANOTHUS
Ceanothus fendleri
Buckthorn family (Rhamnaceae)

Description: Numerous bright white flowers make up the showy umbrella-shaped clusters of this low, spiny shrub. Star-shaped blossoms have 5 triangular sepals, 5 spoon-shaped petals, and 5 pink stamens that are attached in front of the petals and topped with black and/or green anthers. Small evergreen leaves are entire, toothless, and have 3 obvious parallel veins. Narrow, dark green, alternate leaves are less than 1¼" long. Hidden thorns up to 2" long sit at the end of branches. This shrub commonly grows 4–20" tall, but may reach up to 3'. It usually spreads more wide than high and often grows in clumps.

Bloom Season: June to August

Habitat/Range: Fairly common in coniferous forests, open areas, and dry slopes in the foothill and montane ecosystems from Wyoming to New Mexico.

Comments: Also called Fendler buckthorn or buckbrush. Wildlife browse on this shrub, and butterflies and bees drink the flower's nectar. Navajo Indians ate the inner bark and created an infusion and poultice that helped with nervousness.

CHRIS KASSAR / INSET STEVE OLSON

SERVICEBERRY
Amelanchier alnifolia
Rose family (Rosaceae)

Description: This shrub bears numerous axillary clusters of white blossoms 1–2" wide. The fragrant, star-shaped flowers have 5 narrow petals and many stamens. Twigs and leaves are hairy when young and become smooth as they mature. The alternate ¾–2" long leaves are oval or roundish and broadest near the tip, which is toothed. The dark bluish-purple fruit is sweet and juicy. This upright, sometimes spreading shrub with arching branches grows 3–18' tall.

Bloom Season: April to June

Habitat/Range: Found on slopes, in open forests, and near streams in the foothills and montane ecosystems from Alaska to New Mexico.

Comments: Also called saskatoon, Juneberry (the berries ripen then), or shadbush (the flowers bloomed in sync with the East Coast shad fish run). Native Americans ate the berries raw or dried them for use as a winter food. The name serviceberry refers to the fact that Eastern settlers used these very early spring flowers in burial services once the ground thawed enough to allow for the burial of those who died in winter.

CHRIS KASSAR

MOUNTAIN DRYAD
Dryas punctata ssp. *hookeriana*
Synonym: *D.octopetala* ssp. *hookeriana*
Rose family (Rosaceae)

Description: Creamy white, saucer-shaped, 1" wide blossoms usually have 8 ovate petals; 8 sticky, hairy, pointed sepals; and many yellow stamens. Leathery leaves are ¼–1½" long with small rounded teeth. Leaf edges often roll under, and white hairs cover the lower surface. The numerous seeds have long plumed tails. The woody stems hug the ground and often produce large mats of vegetation. The leafless, hairy flower stalk may be up to 8" high.

Bloom Season: June to August

Habitat/Range: Common on gravelly slopes and windy ridges of the alpine tundra from Alaska to Colorado.

Comments: The name *dryad* refers to wood nymphs, the tiny fairylike creatures who live in oak forests. The plant gets this name because of its miniature oak-like leaves.

CHRIS KASSAR

WILD STRAWBERRY
Fragaria virginiana
Rose family (Rosaceae)

Description: The 5-petaled white flowers are 1" wide with 5 sepals and many stamens. Palmately compound leaves have 3 toothed leaflets. The leaves are smooth, bluish, and have a coating that rubs off; they usually are taller than the hairy flowering stalks. The tooth at the tip of each leaflet is shorter and narrower than the teeth next to it. The plants bear small red strawberries that are very flavorful. The 4" plants have red runners.

Bloom Season: March to August

Habitat/Range: Commonly found in meadows, moist forests, and on hillsides in the foothills, montane, and subalpine ecosystems from Canada to New Mexico.

Comments: The flowers of woodland strawberry (*F. vesca*) are taller than the leaves. In addition, its leaves are bright green, prominently veined, and hairy on the upper surface, and the tooth at the end of the leaflet usually is longer than the teeth next to it.

CHRIS KASSAR

CHOKECHERRY
Prunus virginiana var. *demissa*
Synonym: *Padus virginiana* ssp. *melanocarpa*
Rose family (Rosaceae)

Description: Small, sweet-smelling blossoms are arranged in cylindrical clusters on this shrub. The flowers have 5 white petals and lemany protruding yellow-tipped stamens. Alternate, oval leaves are 1½–5" long and pointed at the tips. The bright green, simple leaves bear small teeth along the edges. The smooth brownish twigs lack thorns. The round fruits are less than ½" across with a cherrylike pit. The reddish-purple to black cherries are edible but sour and grow in hanging clusters. This deciduous shrub grows 10–15'.

Bloom Season: April to July

Habitat/Range: Found in valleys, near streams, along fences, and on hillsides in the foothills and montane ecosystems from Canada to New Mexico.

Comments: Berries are an important food source for birds, bears, and chipmunks. Many tribes depended on the berries; they ate them fresh, dried chokecherry patties for winter use, and brewed tea from the stem and bark. All parts of the plant, except the cherry flesh, are poisonous.

CHRIS KASSAR

BOULDER RASPBERRY
Rubus deliciosus
Synonym: *Oreobatus deliciosus*
Rose family (Rosaceae)

Description: This woody shrub has many showy white blossoms that are 1–3" wide. With 5 petals and many stamens, the solitary flowers look similar to those of *Rosa woodsii* (wild rose). The simple, alternate, 1–2½" wide leaves have 3–5 shallow, rounded lobes with small teeth. The branches lack spines and have light brown bark that splits into flakes on the older growth. The fruit looks like a raspberry but is dry and seedy. This shrub grows 2–5' tall.

Bloom Season: May to August

Habitat/Range: Found on dry hillsides and in rocky areas of the foothills and montane ecosystems of Wyoming, Colorado, and northern New Mexico.

Comments: Thimbleberry (*R. parviflorus*) looks similar but has larger leaves with pointed lobes.

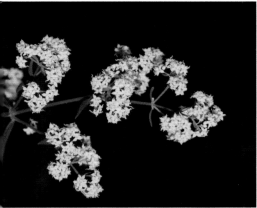

STEVE OLSON

NORTHERN BEDSTRAW
Galium boreale
Synonym: *G. septentrionale*
Madder family (Rubiaceae)

Description: Many tiny, 4-petaled flowers grow in several dense, pyramidal clusters. The sweet-smelling, ⅛" wide blossoms have 4 stamens and no sepals. Narrow leaves are arranged in whorls with 4 leaves per node. The linear to lance-shaped leaves are ¾–2" long with 3 obvious veins. The square stems are erect and usually lack hairs. This perennial grows 8–30" tall.

Bloom Season: May to August

Habitat/Range: Common in meadows, open forests, on hillsides, and near roads in the foothills, montane, and subalpine ecosystems from Alaska to New Mexico.

Comments: Also called cleavers. Pioneers used the dried plants, which retained their loft better than regular straw, to stuff mattresses, hence the common name bedstraw. The generic name *Galium* is the Greek word for "milk"; a related species was used to curdle milk in order to make cheese. This species may be confused with fragrant bedstraw (*G.triflorum*), which has similar flowers but broader leaves in whorls of 6 along its stem.

CHRIS KASSAR

FALSE SOLOMON'S SEAL
Maianthemum racemosum ssp. *amplexicaule*
Synonyms: *M.amplexicaule, Smilacina racemosa*
Butcher's-Broom family (Ruscaceae)

Description: Many tiny white flowers are arranged in a pyramidal, branched cluster (panicle) at the end of a leafy stalk. The blossoms have 6 ovate tepals measuring ⅛" and 6 stamens that are marginally longer. Alternate leaves are 2½–8" long. The ovate leaves have wavy edges and may clasp the stem or have short stalks. The fruit is a ¼" long red berry. The unbranched stem is 1–3' high and often grows in groups.

Bloom Season: March to July

Habitat/Range: Found in moist forests in the foothills, montane, and subalpine ecosystems from Canada to New Mexico.

Comments: Also called Solomon's plume. Can be confused with star Solomonplume (*M. stellatum*), which has 6-pointed starlike flowers growing in long, unbranched clusters (racemes) and narrower leaves with straight edges. Formerly in the Lily family (Liliaceae).

115

CHRIS KASSAR

CHRIS KASSAR

STAR SOLOMONPLUME
Maianthemum stellatum
Synonym: *Smilacina stellata*
Butcher's-Broom family (Ruscaceae)

Description: Usually 3–20 small, star-shaped blossoms grow in long clusters (racemes) at the end of a leafy stem. The ¼" wide flowers have 6 white tepals. Alternate, lance-shaped leaves are up to 6" long. The stalkless, partially folded leaves have pointy tips and straight edges. Immature berries are green with dark stripes turning dark blue or deep purple with age. Erect or somewhat arching stems are 8–24" tall and often grow in groups.

Bloom Season: April to July

Habitat/Range: Found in forests and meadows and near streams in the foothills, montane, and subalpine ecosystems from Alaska to New Mexico.

Comments: Also called star lily, starflower, and star Solomon's seal. Compare to the similar-looking false Solomon's seal (*M. racemosum* ssp. *amplexicaule*) for ways to differentiate. Formerly in the Lily family (Liliaceae). Botanist William Weber puts this plant in the Mayflower family (Convallariaceae).

SNOWBALL SAXIFRAGE
Micranthes rhomboidea
Synonym: *Saxifraga rhomboidea*
Saxifrage family (Saxifragaceae)

Description: Small white flowers are clustered in a round head atop a leafless stalk. The blossoms have 5 petals, 5 sepals, and 10 stamens. Fleshy ¾–3" long leaves grow in a basal rosette. The ovate or diamond-shaped leaves have hairy undersides, toothed edges, and short, wide stalks. The 2–12" flowering stem is covered with sticky hairs.

Bloom Season: May to August

Habitat/Range: Found in meadows and rocky areas in the foothills, montane, subalpine, and alpine ecosystems from Montana to New Mexico.

Comments: Also called diamond-leaf saxifrage. This plant may be confused with American bistort (*Bistorta bistortoides*), which has alternate and basal leaves that are long and narrow.

116

AL SCHNEIDER, WWW.SWCOLORADOWILDFLOWERS.COM

DOTTED SAXIFRAGE
Saxifraga austromontana
Synonym: *Cilaria austromontana*
Saxifrage family (Saxifragaceae)

Description: Several ⅜" wide flowers are borne on slender reddish stalks that have small, alternate leaves. Careful inspection reveals tiny orange and red spots on the slender white petals. These delicate blossoms have 5 sepals and 10 stamens. Mosslike basal leaves have hairs on their edges and a spine at the tip. The leaves are ¼–¾" long. This perennial grows 2–6" tall and often forms mats of vegetation.

Bloom Season: June to August

Habitat/Range: Found on rocky hillsides, boulder fields, open areas, and gravelly slopes of the foothills, montane, subalpine, and alpine ecosystems from Canada to New Mexico.

Comments: Also called spotted saxifrage. *Saxifrage* means "rock breaker," which could refer to the fact that this species often grows in rock crevices. The name could also come from the belief that saxifrage—because it grows in stony areas—had medicinal properties that would dissolve kidney stones.

117

CHRIS KASSAR

CANADA VIOLET
Viola canadensis var. *scopulorum*
Synonym: *V. scopulorum*
Violet family (Violaceae)

Description: Small 5-petaled white flowers with a yellow throat arise from the leaf axils. The back sides of the blossoms are pinkish purple. The 3 lower petals are usually marked with fine purple lines, and the lowest petal has a spur at the tip. Heart-shaped leaves are ¾–2" long and dark green. The leaves are entire or have finely toothed edges and a narrow tip. The leafy stems are 4–12" tall and usually smooth.

Bloom Season: April to July

Habitat/Range: Found on shady, moist hillsides and in canyons in the foothills and montane ecosystems in Colorado and New Mexico.

Comments: *Scopulorum* is Latin for "rocky places." Rydberg violet (*V. canadensis* var. *rugulosa*, formerly *V. rydbergii*) has a hairy stem and hairs on the inner surface of the side petals. As its name implies, the stemless kidneyleaf violet (*V. renifolia*) has kidney-shaped leaves. Swamp white violet (*V. macloskey* ssp. *pallens*) is stemless and grows in wet areas.

This section includes flowers ranging from bright golden yellow and yellow-orange to pale, creamy yellow. Because yellow flowers grade into red, pink, and white flowers, readers looking for yellow flowers should check the red and orange, pink, and white sections as well.

AL SCHNEIDER, WWW.SWCOLORADOWILDFLOWERS.COM

MOUNTAIN PARSLEY

Cymopterus lemmonii
Synonym: *Pseudocymopterus montanus*
Parsley family (Apiaceae)

Description: Tiny yellow flowers are grouped in wide, round to flat-topped clusters up to 2" across. There is 1 main cluster per stem. Some of the green secondary bracts may extend past the edge of the flower cluster. There are a few smooth linear basal leaves with long stalks. The leaves are divided finely and pinnately. The lobes of the leaflets are about ⅛" wide and taper at each end. The small fruits are winged. The plants grow 8–31" in height.

Bloom Season: June to August

Habitat/Range: Found in fields and aspen forests and on rocky hillsides in the foothills, montane, subalpine, and alpine ecosystems from Wyoming to New Mexico.

Comments: Very similar to whiskbroom parsley (*Harbouria trachypleura*), but *H. trachypleura* has stiff basal leaves, secondary bracts that usually do not extend past the edge of the flower cluster, leaflet lobes that do not taper at both ends, and fruits that lack wings. Also compare to alpine parsley (*Oreoxis alpina*), a dwarf alpine plant up to 4" tall. On Pikes Peak, it is replaced by *O. humilis*, which grows nowhere else in the world.

NATIONAL PARK SERVICE

HEARTLEAF ARNICA

Arnica cordifolia
Aster family (Asteraceae)

Description: From 6–13 yellow ray flowers surround many disk flowers clustered in a central button. Each flower petal is notched at the tip, and the showy blossoms measure 2½" or wider. Each stem usually holds a solitary flower, but occasionally holds up to 3 heads. Below the 1–3 heads are hairy bracts. As the specific name implies, the lower leaves are heart-shaped. The largest leaves are up to 5" long and found on separate shoots. The opposite stem leaves are velvety. The upper leaves are ovate and without stalks. Hairy stems grow 4–24" tall.

Bloom Season: May to August

Habitat/Range: Found in coniferous or aspen forests of the foothills, montane, and subalpine ecosystems from Canada to New Mexico.

Comments: Also called leopard's bane. Colonists applied a tincture made from this plant to soothe sprains and cuts. Today arnicas are often used in creams for sore muscles. Some children who have ingested this plant have gone into comas.

SCOTT F. SMITH

STEVE OLSON

FRINGED SAGEWORT
Artemisia frigida
Aster family (Asteraceae)

Description: Tiny yellow disk flowers are arranged in loose, narrow clusters along leafy stems. The ¼" blossoms face out from the stem or may be slightly nodding. The leaves are deeply divided several times into short, very narrow segments; they are light green and covered in short, silvery hairs. Basal leaves appear in clumps; leaves along the stems are alternate. Branched stems are woody at the base. This hairy-stemmed perennial grows 4–16" tall.

Bloom Season: July to October

Habitat/Range: Common in meadows, open forests, on hillsides, and near roads and trails in the foothills, montane, and subalpine ecosystems from Alaska to New Mexico.

Comments: Also called prairie sagewort, mountain sage, or silver sage. This species was first collected in Siberia in 1803, hence, the species name *frigida*, meaning "cold" in Latin. *Artemisias* are easy to recognize due to their silvery-green foliage and the pungent smell of the crushed leaves. They are not related to the sage you cook with (*Salvia officinalis*), which is in the Mint family (Lamiaceae).

ARROWLEAF BALSAMROOT
Balsamorhiza sagittata
Aster family (Asteraceae)

Description: A single yellow sunflower-like head usually sits atop a stout stalk. The flowering stalks bear only a handful of small leaves. Underneath the 2–4½" wide blossoms are woolly bracts. Numerous 8–16" long, entire, arrow-shaped leaves are on long stalks, and they are covered with silvery, woolly hairs. This perennial grows 8–32" tall.

Bloom Season: April to July

Habitat/Range: Found in valleys, open forests, and on slopes in the foothills and montane ecosystems from Canada to Colorado. Hundreds of these plants may color fields and hillsides a brilliant yellow.

Comments: Native Americans ate the young shoots and leaves as well as the roots and seeds. The root (*rhiza* in Greek), which has a balsam-like taste, was used as a poultice for wounds and brewed in a tea for treatment of colds and stomachaches. In Latin, *sagittata*, similar to Sagittarius, the legendary archer, means "arrow," which aptly describes the shape of the leaves.

LORAINE YEATTS

RABBITBRUSH
Ericameria nauseosa var.*graveolens*
Synonym: *Chrysothamnus nauseosus* var. *graveolens*
Aster family (Asteraceae)

Description: Spreading clusters of tiny yellow blossoms crown this shrub. The slender, ¼–½" long flower heads have only disk flowers with smooth yellowish bracts. The alternate, entire leaves are very narrow. Some of the leaves, which are grayish, have 3–5 veins. Slender, branched, flexible stems are light green and covered with dense, matted woolly hairs. This perennial usually grows 2–5' tall but can reach 7'.

Bloom Season: August to October

Habitat/Range: Found in fields, open forests, disturbed areas, and along roads in the foothills from Montana to New Mexico.

Comments: Natives boiled mature flowers to make a yellow dye for wool and baskets. Compare to green rabbitbrush (*Chrysothamnus viscidiflorus*), which lacks the white felt covering on the stems of *E. nauseosa* and instead has brittle, hairless or barely hairy stems, twisted leaves, and sticky flowers. Green rabbitbrush grows from the foothills to subalpine zones.

CHRIS KASSAR

BLANKETFLOWER
Gaillardia aristata
Aster family (Asteraceae)

Description: Resembling a red-eyed sunflower, this *Gaillardia* is one of the showiest blossoms of the Rockies. The yellow ray flowers have 3-lobed tips, and their bases are often colored with red. Flower heads are up to 3½" across. Reddish-purple disk flowers form a ball ¾–2¼" wide at the center of the flower head. The very hairy, stiff, lance-shaped leaves are 2–8" long and may be entire or toothed. One or more hairy stems grow 8–36" in height.

Bloom Season: May to September

Habitat/Range: Found in meadows and on dry hillsides in the foothills and montane ecosystems from Canada to New Mexico.

Comments: Also called gaillardia, brown-eyed Susan, or Indian blanket. A similar species, pinnate-leaf blanketflower (*G. pinnatifida*), is a perennial of the Southern Rockies that has deeply divided leaves. Firewheel (*G. pulchella*) is an annual with reddish ray flowers tipped with yellow.

ERNIE MARX

CHRISTINA MACLEOD

CURLY-CUP GUMWEED
Grindelia squarrosa
Aster family (Asteraceae)

Description: Numerous tiny yellow flower heads grow in flat-topped clusters on top of a leafy plant with branched, erect stems. Blossoms are 1½" wide and have 25–40 rays surrounding a central disk. Multiple overlapping rows of sticky bracts with tips that curl backward and feel rough or scaly grow below the flowers. Leaves are oblong, clasping, toothed and up to 3" long. This aromatic herb grows up to 3' tall.

Bloom Season: July to September

Habitat/Range: Found in dry open sites, roadsides, fields, and disturbed areas in the foothills from Canada to New Mexico.

Comments: Native tribes and early missionaries treated poison ivy, coughing, and congestion with this plant. Because of their antispasmodic and expectorant qualities, extracts continue to be used in modern medicine to relieve asthma and bronchitis. *Grindelia* honors David Hieronymus Grindel (1776–1836), considered the first Latvian natural scientist, doctor, and pharmacist. *Squarrosa* means "with spreading or recurved parts," in reference to the unique bracts.

ASPEN SUNFLOWER
Helianthella quinquenervis
Aster family (Asteraceae)

Description: A single nodding head usually sits atop the stem, although there may be some smaller heads below. Heads have up to 20 light yellow ray flowers and deep yellow to reddish-brown disk flowers. Below the 2–4" wide heads are bracts with hairy margins. Basal leaves are up to 19" long and lance shaped. Stem leaves typically grow in 4 pairs of opposite, leathery leaves. The leaves are prominently 5-veined. Clusters of unbranched stems grow 1–4' in height.

Bloom Season: June to August

Habitat/Range: Commonly found in aspen forests, in meadows, and on hillsides in the foothills, montane, and subalpine ecosystems from Montana to New Mexico.

Comments: Also called 5-nerved, nodding, or little sunflower. In Latin, *quinquenervis* means "5-nerved" and refers to the leaf veins.

AL SCHNEIDER, WWW.SWCOLORADOWILDFLOWERS.COM

AL SCHNEIDER, WWW.SWCOLORADOWILDFLOWERS.COM

ANNUAL SUNFLOWER
Helianthus annuus
Aster family (Asteraceae)

Description: Many large sunflowers grow from the tall, leafy stems of this annual. Ray flowers are yellow with brownish or reddish-purple disk flowers. Below the 3–5" wide heads are bracts rimmed by stiff hairs. Most leaves are alternate and rough. The lower leaves are 2–10" long, heart shaped or ovate, and may be entire or toothed. Hairy stems are branched above and grow 1–13' in height. Clusters may spread 4' wide.

Bloom Season: June to September

Habitat/Range: Abundant in fields, disturbed areas, and along roads in the foothills and montane ecosystems from Canada to New Mexico.

Comments: Also called common sunflower or mirasol. According to Lewis and Clark, Native Americans who lived along the Missouri River used the seeds to thicken soup and as an ingredient in bread. Natives also enjoyed the fruits, got fiber from the stems, and used the flowers to make yellow dye. This species hybridizes with the smaller plains sunflower (*H. petiolaris*).

GOLDEN ASTER
Heterotheca villosa
Synonym: *Chrysopsis villosa*
Aster family (Asteraceae)

Description: Several flower heads, ½–1" wide, sit atop a branched, leafy stem. Both ray and disk flowers are yellow. Usually the bracts below the flower head are leafy. The alternate leaves are lance shaped or narrowly oblong and hairy. Lower leaves have stems while the upper leaves do not. The leaves are ½–2¾" long. The plants, which have more than 1 stem that is covered with short gray hairs, grow 8–20" tall. The seeds are crested with white bristles.

Bloom Season: June to September

Habitat/Range: Very common on hillsides, in open areas, and along roads in the foothills and montane ecosystems from Canada to New Mexico.

Comments: The specific name *villosa* means "with soft hairs." The similar-looking dwarf golden aster (*H. pumila*) thrives on rocky slopes in subalpine and alpine ecosystems. In this case, "dwarf" is a misnomer; this species grows over 1' tall and often has larger flowers and leaves than *H. villosa*.

125

CHRIS KASSAR

OLD MAN OF THE MOUNTAIN
Hymenoxys grandiflora
Synonyms: *Rydbergia grandiflora, Tetraneuris grandiflora*
Aster family (Asteraceae)

Description: These large yellow sunflowers look like giants compared to the other tiny tundra wildflowers. Each stem bears a single, nodding flower head 2–4" wide. Yellow rays have 3 tiny lobes at the tips. Woolly bracts protect the flower buds from harsh alpine weather. The mainly basal leaves are 3–4" long, hairy, and either pinnately divided or divided into slender segments. The stout, woolly stems are 1–12" tall.

Bloom Season: June to August

Habitat/Range: May be abundant on dry hillsides, in meadows, and on windy ridges on the alpine tundra from Montana to New Mexico.

Comments: Also called alpine sunflower or Rydbergia. Flower heads face east throughout the entire day, earning this showy tundra plant the name compass flower. The generic name *Rydbergia* is a tribute to the botanist Per Axel Rydberg, who studied the flora of the Rockies.

BLACK-EYED SUSAN
Rudbeckia hirta
Aster family (Asteraceae)

Description: A dome of dark brown to black disk flowers stands out against yellow or light orange ray flowers. The sunflower-like heads are up to 3" across. Lower leaves are lance shaped while the upper leaves are narrower. Hairy, alternate leaves are up to 6" long. The simple leaves may be entire or have some shallow teeth. This perennial grows up to 30" in height.

Bloom Season: June to August

Habitat/Range: Commonly found in meadows, aspen forests, on slopes, and near trails in the foothills and montane ecosystems from Canada to New Mexico.

Comments: This species, originally from the eastern United States, has spread widely in the West. The generic name honors Olaus Rudbeck, a 17th-century Swedish physician and botany professor; it also honors his son, Olaus Rudbeck Jr.

GOLDENGLOW
Rudbeckia laciniata var.*ampla*
Synonym: *R. ampla*
Aster family (Asteraceae)

Description: Yellow ray flowers, 1–2" long, droop from a cone-shaped mound of dull yellow or greenish-brown disk flowers. The flower heads may be 3–5" across. The long-stalked lower leaves are 3–8" long and divided into 3–7 toothed lobes. The alternate upper leaves are entire or 3-lobed. The branched stems grow 2–6½' tall.

Bloom Season: June to September

Habitat/Range: Common in moist meadows, aspen forests, and along streamsides in the foothills and montane ecosystems from Montana to New Mexico.

Comments: Also called tall coneflower and cutleaf coneflower. Linnaeus named this plant for the Rudbecks, a father and son team who were each physicians, professors, and botanists. Olaus Rudbeck Jr. housed Linnaeus when he was young and provided him financial support for a time.

AL SCHNEIDER, WWW.SWCOLORADOWILDFLOWERS.COM

BLACKTIP SENECIO
Senecio atratus
Aster family (Asteraceae)

Description: Yellow ray flowers and orange disk flowers are arranged in clusters atop a hairy stem. The flower heads have 3–5 rays and are ½" across. Under the flower heads are 8 black-tipped bracts with fuzzy bases. The stalked, nearly vertical basal leaves are 4–8" long and oblong. Alternate, stalkless stem leaves are lance shaped and smaller at the top of the stem. The woolly leaves are grayish green and often have tiny teeth. This stout perennial plant grows in clumps 12–31" tall.

Bloom Season: June to September

Habitat/Range: Common on gravelly hillsides and along roads in the montane and subalpine ecosystems of Utah, Wyominng, Colorado, and New Mexico.

Comments: *Senecio* comes from the Latin *senes* ("old man") and refers to the hairy white bristles attached to the seeds. *Atratus* means "clothed in black," referring to the black-tipped bracts that sit below the yellow flower petals. Some other senecios also have black-tipped bracts, but those of *S. atratus* lack very hairy leaves and stems. Wooton senecio (*S. wootonii*) has leaves with a whitish coating and a winged leaf stalk. Thickbract senecio (*S. crassulus*) has stalkless upper stem leaves that clasp the stem.

CHRIS KASSAR

AL SCHNEIDER, WWW.SWCOLORADOWILDFLOWERS.COM

LAMBSTONGUE GROUNDSEL

Senecio integerrimus
Aster family (Asteraceae)

Description: Typically 5–30 flower heads ¼–¾" wide grow atop slender, upright stems. Both ray flowers and disk flowers are yellow with red-to-black tipped bracts. The stalk of the central flower head is often shorter than the stalk of other flower heads. The leaves have wavy margins or small teeth. Leaves are mainly basal, thick, and 2–6" long. Stem leaves are few, alternate, clasping, and usually smaller. White cobwebby hairs cover leaves and stems but may fall off with age. The stout stems are 8–28" tall.

Bloom Season: March to July

Habitat/Range: Found in meadows, open forests, along roadsides, and on slopes in the foothills, montane, and subalpine ecosystems from Canada to northern New Mexico.

Comments: Also called early spring senecio, butterweed, or ragwort.

TRIANGULARLEAF SENECIO

Senecio triangularis
Aster family (Asteraceae)

Description: Eight yellow ray flowers surround yellow disk flowers in heads 1–1½" across. Numerous flower heads grow in wide, branching, flat-topped clusters. The usually hairy bracts below the flower head are the same length and in 1 row, except for a few shorter bracts at the bottom. Alternate, triangular leaves are 2–8" long, coarsely toothed, and mainly smooth. The stout, leafy stems usually are smooth. The plants often grow in clumps and reach 1–5' tall.

Bloom Season: June to September

Habitat/Range: Abundant along streamsides and in moist open woods, swamps, and other wet areas in the montane, subalpine, and alpine ecosystems from Alaska to New Mexico.

Comments: Compare to *S. serra* (tall ragwort), which shares similar habitat and many characteristics but has leaves that are tapered at the base, not squared like the triangular leaves of *S. triangularis*. *S. triangularis* leaves are shallowly saw-toothed, while the leaves of *S. serra* are finely serrated.

129

AL SCHNEIDER, WWW.SWCOLORADOWILDFLOWERS.COM

LORAINE YEATTS

NORTHERN GOLDENROD

Solidago multiradiata
Aster family (Asteraceae)

Description: Dense, rounded terminal clusters of tiny yellow flowers sit atop reddish stems. Numerous (12–18) rays surround a tightly packed center of 10–35 yellow disc florets. Flowers are ¼–½" across. Leaves are mainly basal, spoon shaped, toothed, and smooth; leaf stalks, however, are fringed with hairs. Stem leaves are few and smaller. Plants usually grow to 1' tall, but can reach 3'.

Bloom Season: July to September

Habitat/Range: Open areas, woodlands, slopes, meadows, and tundra in foothills to subalpine ecosystems from Alaska to New Mexico.

Comments: Also known as Rocky Mountain goldenrod or alpine goldenrod. This plant has been used for its healing powers for generations. Goldenrod tea relieves intestinal distress and cramps. The generic name, *Solidago*, comes from *solidus*, which means "whole," and *ago*, meaning "to make," referring to its medicinal properties and ability to make a sick person whole again.

STEMLESS FOUR-NERVE DAISY

Tetraneuris acaulis
Synonym: *Hymenoxys acaulis*
Aster family (Asteraceae)

Description: One showy yellow flower sits atop each short leafless stalk growing from a tuft of woolly basal leaves. The 1–2" wide head has many disk flowers surrounded by 8–13 broad rays, each of which has 3 notches at the tip. Overlapping rows of broad, hairy phyllaries sit below the blossom. Silvery basal leaves are simple, linear to lance shaped, and have varying amounts of hair. This highly variable species often grows in clumps and may reach 1–16" tall.

Bloom Season: May to September

Habitat/Range: Found in open, dry areas, rocky places, and hillsides in the foothills, montane, and subalpine zones from Canada to New Mexico.

Comments: There are at least 4 varieties of *T. acaulis*, making this common species highly variable. In Greek, *tetraneuris* means "4 nerves," and *acaulis* means "lacking leaves on the stem."

CHRIS KASSAR

CHRIS KASSAR

SALSIFY
Tragopogon dubius
Aster family (Asteraceae)

Description: This dandelion look-alike has a single lemon-yellow flower head atop a stem 1–3' tall. The heads are 1–2" or more across and have only ray flowers. From 10–13 green, pointed phyllaries grow longer than the ray flowers. Grasslike leaves 5–6" long clasp the stem. Hollow stems are branched near the base and enlarged below the flower. Sap is milky. Numerous seeds with little parachutes form a round seed head that is 2–4" in diameter.

Bloom Season: May to August

Habitat/Range: Found in meadows and along roadsides in the foothills and montane ecosystems from Canada to New Mexico.

Comments: Also called goat's beard; *tragos* is Greek for "goat" and *pogon* for "beard." A nonnative originally from Europe but now widely established across the United States. This species looks like meadow salsify (*T. pratensis*), which has purple-margined phyllaries that are not longer than the ray flowers.

OREGON GRAPE
Mahonia repens
Synonym: *Berberis repens*
Barberry family (Berberidaceae)

Description: Groups of small yellow flowers, each with 6 petals, 6 sepals, and 6 stamens, grow in elongated clusters along this low shrub. The alternate, pinnately compound leaves have 3–7 evergreen leaflets, which are spiny, 3" long, and holly-like. The ovate leathery leaflets often turn red in the fall. The juicy, dark purple-blue berries have a whitish powdery covering and a few seeds. Plants grow to 10" tall and can spread 3–4' wide.

Bloom Season: April to June

Habitat/Range: Found on dry slopes and in forests of the foothills and montane ecosystems from Canada to New Mexico.

Comments: Also called mountain holly, creeping hollygrape, or creeping mahonia. The specific name *repens* means "creeping," referring to the way the plant spreads from underground stems.

131

CHARLIE & JAN TURNER

NATIONAL PARK SERVICE

MANY-FLOWERED PUCCOON

Lithospermum multiflorum
Borage family (Boraginaceae)

Description: Bright yellow trumpet-shaped
flowers grow in compact clusters at the tip of the
stem. The flowers have tubular throats and 5 round
petals that lack fringes and measure 1¼" across.
Leaves are narrow, slightly toothed, alternate,
1–2" long, and grow tightly packed along the stem.
The upper part of this plant is branched, and its
stems often lean outward in many directions. Few
to numerous stems grow 9–24" tall.

Bloom Season: May to August

Habitat/Range: Found in meadows, open forests,
and on hillsides in the foothills, montane, and subalpine ecosystems from Wyoming to New Mexico.

Comments: Also called many-flowered stoneseed
or gromwell. The larger blossoms of narrowleaf
puccoon (*L. incisum*) have fringed petal edges,
longer tubes, and a narrower throat opening. *Lithospermum* means "stone seed," which refers to the
hard nutlets that are the fruits, and *puccoon* comes
from an Algonquian word denoting plants use for
dye or paint. Native Americans used the roots to
make a purple dye.

GOLDEN DRABA

Draba aurea
Mustard Family (Brassicaceae)

Description: Yellow, 4-petaled flowers have
6 stamens and 4 green, hairy sepals with pale
margins. Styles are ⅟₁₆" long or less. The small,
cross-shaped flowers cluster at the top of slender
stems. Basal leaves are ¼–2" long and arranged
in a rosette. A few nearly vertical leaves clasp the
stem. Leaves are variable in size and edging, but
they are usually covered with fine hairs, oval or
spoon shaped, and entire. Narrow seedpods are
flat or twisted, and fruits are up to ½" long. These
gray-green plants usually grow in clumps and 2–6"
tall, though they can reach 20" at times.

Bloom Season: June to August

Habitat/Range: Abundant in fields, rock outcrops,
dry pine forests, and on hillsides or tundra in the
montane, subalpine, and alpine ecosystems from
Alaska to New Mexico.

Comments: Great variability between and within
species adds to the challenge of identifying the
numerous species of small yellow or white flowered plants in this genus. The taller spectacular or
showy draba (*D. spectabilis*) has toothed leaves
and tends to be bright green because it is hairless
or less hairy than *D. aurea*. Twisted-fruit draba
(*D. streptocarpa*) has fruits that are strongly twisted
and coarse hairs on its basal leaves. It grows
primarily in Colorado but has also been found in
Wyoming and New Mexico.

CHRIS KASSAR

WESTERN WALLFLOWER
Erysimum capitatum
Mustard family (Brassicaceae)

Description: Fragrant flowers in a showy, ball-like cluster typically are yellow, orange, or maroon (sometimes lavender or brownish). The 4 petals are more than ¼" long, with the blossoms up to 1" wide. Narrow 1–5" long leaves are basal or alternate, covered with rough hairs, and usually have small teeth. The slender, 2–4" long pods stand upright and are nearly vertical (almost parallel to the stem). This highly variable species can grow 6–36" in height with few or no branches.

Bloom Season: April to September

Habitat/Range: Found in meadows, pine forests, and on gravelly hillsides in the foothills, montane, subalpine, and alpine ecosystems from Canada to New Mexico.

Comments: Also called prairie rocket. A similar, but exotic, montane species, treacle wallflower or wormseed mustard (*E. cheiranthoides*) has yellow flowers with shorter petals and bears a fruit less than 1¼" long.

NATIONAL PARK SERVICE BY RUSSELL SMITH

CHRIS KASSAR

PLAINS PRICKLY PEAR

Opuntia polyacantha
Cactus family (Cactaceae)

Description: Large, showy flowers commonly are yellow but may be pink and often fade to a copper color. The 2–3" wide blossoms have many shiny petals and numerous stamens. Flowers are borne at the edge of the pads. The jointed, oval stems flatten into very spiny, but unwrinkled pads that grow 2–6" long and bear small bristles. There are 3–10 spines per cluster; the rigid spines are 2–3" long. The edible, oval fruit is ¾–1½" long, spiny, and tan. These spreading plants are 3–8" tall.

Bloom Season: April to July

Habitat/Range: Grows in dry, sunny areas of the foothills ecosystem from Canada to New Mexico.

Comments: Also called hunger cactus or starvation prickly pear because its dry fruits were a last-chance food choice. The fleshy fruits of twisted spine prickly pear (*O. macrorhiza*) were preferred. Fragile prickly pear (*O. fragilis*) has rounder stems. Several Great Plains Indian nations used the mucilaginous juice of prickly pears to waterproof and preserve painted designs on leather. These species are highly variable, and they hybridize, making positive identification difficult at times. *Polyacantha* means "many spines."

TWINBERRY

Lonicera involucrate
Synonym: *Distegia involucrata*
Honeysuckle family (Caprifoliaceae)

Description: Pale yellow to greenish (sometimes pinkish) tubular flowers are seated in a conspicuous cup of maroon bracts. Flowers are ⅓–1" long and hang in opposite pairs from leaf axils. Broad, large bracts turn deep red as the flower fades. Simple, opposite, ovate leaves are 2–6" long, hairy, and pointed. Shiny pairs of juicy but inedible and possibly poisonous black to purple berries have pairs of reddish, backward-spreading bracts. This common and colorful deciduous shrub often grows 3–6' tall, but can reach 9'.

Bloom Season: March to July

Habitat/Range: Found along streams, on moist slopes, or in forests from the foothills to subalpine ecosytems from Canada to New Mexico.

Comments: Also called bush or bracted honeysuckle. The berries taste awful and may cause illness if ingested. *Lonicera* honors German physician and herbalist Adam Lonicer (1528–1586). In Latin, *involucrata* means "wrapper" and refers to the distinctive involucre, or group of bracts at the base of this flower cluster.

CHRIS KASSAR   AL SCHNEIDER, WWW.SWCOLORADOWILDFLOWERS.COM

YELLOW STONECROP

Sedum lanceolatum ssp. *lanceolatum*
Synonym: *Amerosedum lanceolatum*
Stonecrop family (Crassulaceae)

Description: Flat-topped clusters of 5–25 yellow, star-shaped flowers sit atop fleshy stems. The blossoms are ¼–½" wide with 5 lance-shaped and pointed petals, 4–5 sepals, and 8–10 stamens. Narrow, succulent leaves form tight basal rosettes. The green or reddish-brown leaves are ¼–¾" long. The alternate, unstalked stem leaves are smooth with a waxy coating to retain moisture. This perennial grows to 8" tall.

Bloom Season: June to August

Habitat/Range: Common on dry, rocky sites in the foothills, montane, subalpine, and alpine ecosystems from Canada to New Mexico.

Comments: Many say that the young flowers, leaves, and stems are edible raw, however, they have caused stomach sickness and headaches so we suggest enjoying them from afar. Due to their succulent leaves, they are very drought resistant and well suited for their rocky habitat. *S.lanceolatum* is a host plant for the Phoebus Parnassian butterfly, a 2–3" white critter with black and red spots and dark gray markings that absorb more heat, helping it to thrive at altitude, much like stonecrop does.

MOUNTAIN GOLDEN BANNER

Thermopsis montana var. *montana*
Bean family (Fabaceae)

Description: The long, showy racemes of these large, yellow flowers are hard to miss. Blossoms resemble pea or lupine flowers and have 10 stamens with separate filaments. Palmately compound leaves have 3 leaflets that are 2–4" long and ¼–1¼" wide. Leaflets are elliptic to lanceolate or oblong. Linear, slender stipules measuring ½–1¼" long are found where the leaves join the stem. Seedpods are slender, erect, and hairy. The plants, which reach 1–2½' tall, have erect branching stems and often grow in groups.

Bloom Season: April to July

Habitat/Range: Common on hillsides, coniferous forest openings, moist sites, meadows, and along streams in the montane and subalpine zones from Montana to New Mexico.

Comments: Also called false lupine because of the similarity between flowers. The similarity is so great that even the scientific name recognizes it; *thermos* is Greek for "lupine," and *opsis* is Greek for "similar." The shorter *T. rhombifolia* (prairie golden banner) has large, leaflike stipules and flattened down-curved pods that often arc into a half circle. The pods of *T. divicarpa* (spreadfruit golden banner) are straight or slightly curved and spreading, and its stipules are broader and ovate than those of *T. montana*.

LORAINE YEATTS

CHRIS KASSAR

GOLDEN SMOKE

Corydalis aurea
Fumitory family (Fumariaceae)

Description: Clusters of yellow, spurred, tubelike flowers lie amid lacy, fernlike leaves. The ½–¾" long, 4-petaled blossoms have 2 outer petals (the upper one is spurred) and 2 inner petals that are joined at the top. There are 2 tiny sepals, which fall off early, and 6 stamens. Smooth 3–6" long leaves are twice pinnately divided. Narrow, slightly curved pods are ¾–1" long. This branched 4–16" plant usually grows in low clumps.

Bloom Season: March to August

Habitat/Range: Found on gravelly slopes, dis-turbed ground, and along streams and roads in the foothills, montane, and lower subalpine ecosys-tems from Alaska to New Mexico.

Comments: Also called scrambled eggs. This plant could be easily mistaken for a member of the pea family (Fabaceae), but it is in the Fumitory family (Fumariaceae) and is related to western bleeding heart (*Dicentra formosa*), Dutchman's breeches (*D. cucullaria*), steershead (*D. uniflora*), and squirrel corn (*D. canadensis*). *Corydalis* is the Greek word for the crested lark bird, a species with a spur on its foot. The genus name could refer to the hood of the upper petal or to the spur of the flower. In Latin, *aurea* means "golden."

GLACIER LILY

Erythronium grandiflorum
Lily family (Liliaceae)

Description: Exquisite bright yellow blossoms with curved-back tepals dangle from slender stems. Usually 1 flower (sometimes 2 or 3) grows on each smooth stalk. Six showy golden or red stamens protrude from the center of the 6-narrow tepals that form the blossoms. The 2 smooth basal leaves are 4–8" long. The shiny green leaves are oblong and have parallel veins. The fruit is a 3-sided capsule. These showy plants often grow in groups and are 6–15" tall.

Bloom Season: April to August

Habitat/Range: Found at moist edges of melting snowbanks as well as in meadows, forests, and near streams in the foothills, montane, subalpine, and alpine ecosystems from Canada to Colorado.

Comments: Also called avalanche, snow or fawn lily, adder's-tongue, or dogtooth violet. Members of many different Native American nations cooked and ate the bulbs.

NATIONAL PARK SERVICE

MARY DUBLER

YELLOW PONDLILY

Nuphar polysepala
Synonym: *N. lutea* ssp. *polysepala*
Water Lily family (Nymphaeaceae)

Description: Waxy, cup-shaped yellow flowers are 3–5½" wide. Blossoms have 5–12 yellow sepals, which may be tinted with green or red. From 10–20 true petals are smaller than the sepals and the same length as the many reddish-purple stamens. Numerous pistils share a fleshy base. Flowers are on stalks just above the water, or they float on the water's surface like the leathery leaves. The simple, entire leaves are oval, round, or heart shaped, 4–12" long, with serpentlike underwater stalks that can be more than 40" long. This perennial has a somewhat egg-shaped fruit that is 1" in diameter.

Bloom Season: May to August

Habitat/Range: Found sporadically in montane and subalpine ponds, lakes, and calmer streams from Alaska to Colorado.

Comments: Also called spatterdock or wokas. Klamath Indians ate the roasted seeds or made bread and porridge from the ground seeds. Moose eat the leathery leaves, and beavers and muskrats eat the scaly yellow roots.

COMMON EVENING PRIMROSE

Oenothera villosa
Evening Primrose family (Onagraceae)

Description: These yellow flowers bloom for 1 evening and then fade to orange. The 4 petals are less than 1" long and open in the late afternoon. The blossoms have 8 stamens, a 4-parted stigma, and 4 bent-back sepals. Alternate 1–4" long leaves are hairy and usually entire. The erect 1–4' stem is covered with stiff hairs.

Bloom Season: June to September

Habitat/Range: Common in disturbed sites and along roads and trails in the foothills and montane ecosystems from Montana to Colorado.

Comments: Formerly known by the scientific name *O. strigosa*, this species is pollinated by moths, night insects, butterflies, and native bees. Yellow evening primrose (*O. flava*) is a very low plant with toothed or lobed leaves and bright flowers that grow 1½–2" across. Hooker's evening primrose (*O.elata*) also resembles *O. villosa*, but *O. elata* is very showy, commonly grows over 3' tall (sometimes to 5'), and its bright yellow flowers are twice as large, reaching 2–3" wide or more.

137

SCOTT F. SMITH

NATIONAL PARK SERVICE

YELLOW LADYSLIPPER

Cypripedium parviflorum var. *pubescens*
Synonym: *C. calceolus*
Orchid family (Orchidaceae)

Description: A single, bright yellow moccasin-shaped flower dangles from an erect stem. This flower has 3 sepals and 3 petals. The yellow lower petal forms a sac-shaped lip and is 2–3" long. The two lateral, reddish-tan or yellowish-green petals are twisted and spiraling. The 2 bottom sepals are joined together, and the back sepal acts as a hood over the top of the lip. Reddish-purple dots mark the inside of this fragrant blossom. There usually are 3–5 alternate, deeply veined leaves that are 3–6" long. Sticky hairs cover the leaves and the stems. The stout, hairy stem reaches 18" tall.

Bloom Season: April to August

Habitat/Range: This rare plant is found in moist aspen forests, in marshes, along streams, and bordering ponds in the foothills, montane, and subalpine ecosystems from Canada to New Mexico.

Comments: Also called large lady's slipper. *C. parviflorum* var. *pubescens* is extremely rare, endangered in some states, including New Mexico, and threatened in other neighboring states.

WESTERN YELLOW PAINTBRUSH

Castilleja occidentalis
Broomrape family (Orobanchaeceae)

Description: Greenish to very light yellow flowers are tucked among showier, hairy bracts that are greenish yellow. Slightly hairy tubular flowers have a small lower lip, a long slender upper lip, and grow in spikes. The lanceolate bracts are entire or may have shallow lobes. The leaves are usually entire, 1–2" long, and lance shaped. Several woolly, unbranched stems often grow together in a clump. Grows 2–10" tall.

Bloom Season: June to September

Haibtat/Range: Common in meadows and on tundra in subalpine and alpine ecosystems of Colorado and New Mexico. Also found (though not common) in Canada, Montana, Idaho, and Utah.

Comments: This species is shorter than the yellow-flowered northern paintbrush (*C. septentrionalis*), but they share a number of similarities. The flowers of alpine paintbrush (*C. puberula*) have a longer lower lip, and the leaves are narrower. *Castilleja* are often pollinated by butterflies, bumblebees, and native bees, and the species in this genus are a major nectar source for the broadtailed hummingbird. Formerly in the Figwort family (Scrophulariaceae).

SCOTT F. SMITH

NORTHERN PAINTBRUSH
Castilleja septentrionalis
Synonym: *C. sulphurea*
Broomrape family (Orobanchaeceae)

Description: Sticky hairs adorn the clusters of pale yellow or whitish sepals and bracts that hide inconspicuous flowers. The 1" long, thin tubular blossoms have an upper yellow petal; the lower petal looks like a green bump. The leaves are 1–3" long, usually smooth and entire, lance shaped, and have 3–5 main veins. The stems are often branched once. The plants are 12–20" tall, but sometimes shorter, and often grow in clumps.

Bloom Season: June to August

Habitat/Range: Common in moist aspen forests, in shady meadows, and near streams in the foothills, montane, and subalpine ecosystems from Canada to New Mexico.

Comments: Also called yellow paintbrush. Identification of species in this genus can be challenging because species hybridize often and colors vary. The similar western yellow paintbrush (*C. occidentalis*) has a shorter, unbranched stem. The yellow-flowered alpine paintbrush (*C. puberula*) is covered with woolly hairs. Formerly in the Figwort family (Scrophulariaceae).

ERNIE MARX

YELLOW OWL'S CLOVER
Orthocarpus luteus
Broomrape family (Orobanchaeceae)

Description: Many small, yellow, tubular flowers grow in spikelike clusters. Blossoms are ¼–½" long with 2 inconspicuous lips and 4 hidden stamens. Flowers are dispersed among short, green, lance-shaped bracts that have 3–5 lobes and are glandular and hairy. Leaves are narrow, alternate, occasionally divided into 3 lobes, and less than 1½" long. The slender stem grows 4–20" tall.

Bloom Season: June to September

Habitat/Range: Found in meadows, fields, and open woods in the foothills and montane ecosystems from Canada to New Mexico.

Comments: This is the most wide-ranging *Orthocarpus*; it grows across most of the West and to the upper Midwest. *Orthocarpus* refers to its straight ("ortho") fruit ("carpus"). In Latin, *luteus* means "yellow." Formerly in the Figwort family (Scrophulariaceae).

NATIONAL PARK SERVICE

STEVE OLSON

BRACTED LOUSEWORT
Pedicularis bracteosa var. *paysoniana*
Broomrape family (Orobanchaeceae)

Description: Many creamy yellow flowers, often with tinges of purple or pink, are arranged in a dense, spikelike cluster with leafy green bracts. The 1" long blossoms are 2-lipped with a longer, arched-and-hooded top lip and a shorter, 3-lobed bottom lip. The stalked, 2–6" long leaves are finely divided into toothed, fernlike leaflets and arranged alternately along the tall hairy stalk. This perennial has several unbranched stems that grow 1–3' tall.

Bloom Season: June to August

Habitat/Range: Found in forests, shady meadows, and on rocky hillsides in the montane, subalpine, and alpine ecosystems from Montana to northern New Mexico.

Comments: Also called wood betony or fernleaf lousewort. Giant lousewort (*P. procera*) has longer leaves and flowers with reddish-purple streaks. The yellow- or reddish-flowered Canada louse-wort (*P. canadensis*) has simple leaves that are not deeply lobed. Formerly in the Figwort family (Scrophulariaceae).

YELLOW MONKEYFLOWER
Mimulus guttatus
Lopseed family (Phrymaceae)

Description: Bright yellow tubular blossoms resemble snapdragons and characterize this highly variable plant. The blossom is ½–1½" long and 2-lipped. The smaller 2-lobed upper lip bends upward, and the hairy 3-lobed lower lip bends downward. There are 2 humps on the lower lip that are covered with yellow hairs and reddish-brown dots. Opposite, ovate, clasping leaves have coarse teeth on the edges and 3–7 veins. Numerous flowers often grow in loose clusters on slender, leafy stems that grow 4–36" tall.

Bloom Season: April to September

Habitat/Range: Grows in wet areas, meadows, along streams, and near seeps in the foothills, montane, and subalpine ecosystems from Canada to New Mexico.

Comments: The blossoms of mountain monkey-flower (*M. tillingi*) are very similar to *M. guttatus*, but the former is a dwarf creeping shrub that grows less than 8" tall and has fewer flowers per stem. Typically it grows in subalpine and alpine meadows and moist areas. Formerly in the Figwort family (Scrophulariaceae).

LORAINE YEATTS

NATIONAL PARK SERVICE

SULPHUR FLOWER
Eriogonum umbellatum
Buckwheat family (Polygonaceae)

Description: Small bright yellow flowers are grouped in ball-like clusters. The clusters sit atop stalks that all originate from 1 point; just below this point are several leafy bracts. Each flower has 6 petal-like sepals that turn reddish brown as they age. A basal rosette contains oval or spoon-shaped leaves that are ¼–2" long with fuzzy hairs on the undersurface. Leaves turn crimson in fall. The small seeds are not winged. This perennial grows 4–12" tall and spreads out 1-2' wide in loose, broad mats.

Bloom Season: May to September

Habitat/Range: This widespread, variable species is found in meadows, fields, forest openings, on slopes, and along roads in the foothills, montane, and subalpine ecosystems from Canada to Colorado.

Comments: Over 50 species of *Eriogonum* bloom in the Rocky Mountains, making identification difficult at times. The generic name *Eriogonum* means "woolly knee," referring to the woolly leaves and swollen stems of some species. *Umbellatum* comes from the flower clusters that look like little umbrellas (also called an umbel).

SNOW BUTTERCUP
Ranunculus adoneus
Buttercup family (Ranunculaceae)

Description: From 1–3 showy yellow, cup-shaped flowers usually appear before the leaves unfurl. The ¾–1½" wide blossoms have shiny petals and hairy sepals. The leaves have 3 lobes, each of which is twice divided into narrow segments. The seed heads are egg shaped. Smooth stems grow 4–12", and the plants often appear in clusters.

Bloom Season: May to September

Habitat/Range: Found circling melting snowbanks, in wet meadows, and near streams in the upper subalpine and alpine ecosystems in Idaho, Montana, Wyoming, Utah, and Colorado.

Comments: Also called alpine buttercup. A similar species, subalpine buttercup (*R. eschscholtzii*) has 3-lobed leaves with entire or once-divided segments and oblong seed heads.

AL SCHNEIDER, WWW.SWCOLORADOWILDFLOWERS.COM

AL SCHNEIDER, WWW.SWCOLORADOWILDFLOWERS.COM

SAGEBRUSH BUTTERCUP

Ranunculus glaberrimus var. *ellipticus*
Buttercup family (Ranunculaceae)

Description: Typically 5–8 shiny yellow petals surround numerous stamens. The ¾–1¼" wide, cup-shaped blossoms have 5 reddish- and/or purple-tinged sepals and bracts with a larger middle lobe. Long-stemmed basal leaves are undivided and round or elliptic. The smooth ½–2" long leaves are entire and fleshy. The stem leaves usually have 3 lobes. This perennial grows to 2–8" in height and usually has a reclining stem.

Bloom Season: March to July

Habitat/Range: Found in fields of sagebrush, on moist hillsides, and in sunny pine forests in the foothills and montane ecosystems from Canada to New Mexico.

Comments: Also called crowfoot or early buttercup, this is one of the first species to bloom in spring. All parts of this plant are poisonous, but they have a low toxicity if eaten. Because the toxin is unstable, boiling or drying leaves neutralizes its effect—but we don't recommend testing this.

SHRUBBY CINQUEFOIL

Dasiphora fruticosa ssp. *floribunda*
Synonyms: *Pentaphylloides floribunda, D. floribunda*
Rose family (Rosaceae)

Description: This shrub is often covered with clusters of 5-petaled yellow blossoms that have many stamens. The 1–1½" wide flowers resemble buttercups and have 5 sepals. The pinnately compound leaves are usually less than 1½" long and divided into 3–7 narrow, elliptical-shaped and entire leaflets. The bark is brownish, peeling, and lacks thorns. The bottom section of the branched stems is woody. This plant usually grows 4–40" tall, sometimes reaching 60".

Bloom Season: June to September

Habitat/Range: Found in moist meadows, open woods, and on hillsides in the foothills, montane, subalpine, and alpine ecosystems from Alaska to New Mexico.

Comments: Also called yellow rose (formerly *Potentilla fruticosa*), varieties of this plant are popular in yards and gardens. *Dasiphora* is Greek for "hair bearing" and may relate to the hairy bark and seeds. Native American tribes have used various parts of this plant for medicinal and ceremonial purposes, including drinking tea made from the leaves. *Potentilla* comes from the Latin *potens* for "powerful" and may denote the medicinal value of some species.

CHRIS KASSAR

LORAINE YEATTS

ALPINE AVENS

Geum rossii var. *turbinatum*
Synonym: *Acomastylis rossii* ssp. *turbinate*
Rose family (Rosaceae)

Description: Bright ¾" wide blossoms have 5 rounded yellow petals, 5 pointed green sepals, and numerous stamens. The blossom is cup shaped, and the sepals are often tinged maroon or purple. Fernlike, 1–8" long leaves are mainly basal. The deep green leaves are pinnately divided into 9–33 toothed leaflets; 1–3 leaves clasp the stem. This 3–10" plant often forms a yellow-and-green carpet on the alpine tundra, but in fall, the leaves blanket the earth in deep red and maroon.

Bloom Season: June to August

Habitat/Range: Very common in meadows and gravelly areas of the subalpine and alpine ecosystems from Montana to New Mexico.

Comments: Also called Ross's avens. The specific name honors the Arctic explorer Captain James Ross, who was the first to collect this plant in 1820 in Canada's Northwest Territories. Cinquefoils *(Potentilla)* look similar, but their basal leaves usually have 3–13 leaflets and may be palmately compound. In addition, *G. rossii*'s flower is cup or funnel shaped, and it has hairy, lanceolate achenes that taper to long, slender styles. Potentilla flowers are nearly flat and often have smooth, egg-shaped achenes.

BEAUTIFUL CINQUEFOIL

Potentilla pulcherrima
Synonym: *P. gracilis* var. *pulcherrima*
Rose family (Rosaceae)

Description: Flat-topped clusters of bright yellow, ½–¾" flowers sit atop branched stems. The 5 petals often are decorated with an orange spot at the base, and the 5 sepals have long white hairs. The mainly basal, handlike leaves have long stalks. They are palmately compound with narrow leaflets that are toothed to the base. The 5–11 leaflets are smooth and green above with white woolly hairs below. Slender stems are 1–2' high.

Bloom Season: June to August

Habitat/Range: Very commonly found in meadows, open forests, on moist hillsides, or near streams in the foothills, montane, and subalpine ecosystems from Alaska to Colorado.

Comments: Also called beauty cinquefoil. William Weber separates these 2 species because, in his opinion, *P. pulcherrima* "differs markedly" from *P. gracilis* in its dense hairiness on the underside of the leaflet. The palmate leaf seen in beautiful cinquefoil (*P. pulcherrima)* is common for members of *Potentilla*, but so is the ladderlike leaf arrangement seen in silvery cinquefoil (*P. hippiana*). *P. hippiana* has silvery, hairy pinnate leaves with toothed leaflets, tufted stems, and flowers that are ½" across. It prefers dry slopes in foothills, montane, and subalpine ecosystems. Another similar species, leafy cinquefoil (*Drymocalis fissa*) grows in narrow, dense cymes and has feather-like, pinnately compound leaves. Cinquefoils may be hard to identify since they interbreed and create hybrids with intermediate characteristics.

143

SCOTT F. SMITH

COMMON ALUMROOT
Heuchera parvifolia
Saxifrage family (Saxifragaceae)

Description: Dainty, pale yellow funnel-shaped flowers grow in panicles (spikelike clusters) on top of a largely leafless stem. Blooms are less than ⅕" with 5 ovate petals that are 1½ times as long as calyx lobes. Thick, bright green basal leaves are broad and heart shaped with blunt or rounded teeth. Glands tipped with hairs cover the top of the tall stem, which can reach 2" tall.

Bloom Season: May to September

Habitat/Range: Found in rocky outcrops, talus slopes, and granitic and limestone cliffs from the foothills to alpine slopes from Canada to New Mexico.

Comments: Natives used *H. parvifolia* root to help ease rheumatism, stomachache, and to help cure sores.

GLOSSARY

Achenes—small, one-seeded fruit containing a single seed; the typical fruit of the Aster family (Asteraceae).

Alternate—placed singly along a stem or axis, one after another, usually each successive item on a different side from the previous; often used in reference to the arrangement of leaves on a stem; see **Opposite** (see illustration p. 9).

Annual—a plant that completes its life cycle—from seed germination to the production of new seeds—within a year and then dies.

Awn—a slender stiff bristle or fiber attached at its base to another part, such as a leaf tip.

Axil—the site where a leaf joins the stem axillary (where the leaf joins the stem)—i.e., axillary clusters.

Banner—the usually erect, spreading upper petal in many flowers of the Bean family (Fabaceae); also called the standard.

Basal—at the base or bottom of; generally used in reference to leaves.

Biennial—a plant that completes its life cycle in two years, normally not producing flowers during the first year.

Boreal—northern.

Bract—reduced or modified leaf, often associated with flowers. May or may not be green; sometimes scalelike.

Bristle—a stiff hair, usually erect or curving away from its attachment point.

Bulb—an underground plant part derived from a short, usually rounded shoot that is covered with scales or leaves.

Calyx—the outer set of flower parts, composed of the sepals, which may be separate or joined together; usually green.

Capsule—a dry fruit that releases seeds through splits or holes.

Ciliate—fringed with cilia, or hairs.

Circumboreal—found around the world in northern regions.

Circumpolar—found around the world in alpine or polar regions.

Clasping—surrounding or partially wrapping around a stem or branch.

Cluster—any grouping or close arrangement of individual flowers; "flower cluster" is used as a substitute for the commonly used but more technical term **Inflorescence.**

Compound leaf—a leaf that is divided into two or more leaflets, each of which may look like a complete leaf but which lacks buds; may have leaflets arranged along an axis, like the rays of a feather, or radiating from a common point, like the fingers on a hand (see illustration p. 9).

Conifer—a cone-bearing tree or shrub, usually evergreen.

Corm—an enlarged base or stem resembling a bulb.

Corolla—the set of flower parts interior to the calyx and surrounding the stamens, composed of petals that may be free or united; often brightly colored.

Cyme—a flat-topped or rounded flower cluster in which the blooms on the inner branches flower first.

Deciduous—trees or shrubs that drop their leaves at the end of each growing season.

Disk flower—small, tubular flowers in the central portion of the flower head of many plants in the Aster family (Asteraceae) (see illustration p. 13).

Dissected—a leaf deeply cut into segments or lobes.

Disturbed—referring to habitats changed by actions or processes associated with human activities such as ditching, grading, or long intervals of high-intensity grazing. There are also naturally disturbed areas changed by snow and rock avalanches, frost heaves, erosion, etc.

Ecosystem—a recognizable community of plants and animals affected by environmental factors such as elevation, wind, temperature, precipitation, sunlight, soil type, and direction of slope.

Elliptical—usually in reference to leaf shape that is oval or oblong with rounded ends and a wider middle (see illustration p. 10).

Endemic—prevalent in or confined to a certain region or ecological niche.

Entire—usually in reference to a leaf margin that is smooth, without teeth or notches (see illustration p. 10).

Erect—upright, standing vertically, or directly perpendicular from a surface.

Evergreen—a plant that retains most of its leaves all year.

Family—a group of related genera, usually easily recognized because they share similar features, such as floral features, flower arrangement, fruit types, and stem anatomy.

Flower head—as used in this guide, a dense and continuous group of flowers without obvious branches or space between them; used especially in reference to the Aster family (Asteraceae).

Genus—a subdivision of a family encompassing a group of closely related species that share many characteristics in common. Examples: *Viola* (violets), *Rosa* (roses), *Penstemon*.

Gland—a bump, projection, or round protuberance, usually colored differently than the object on which it occurs; often sticky or producing sticky or oily secretions.

Herbaceous—fleshy stemmed; not woody.

Hood—a curving or folded petal-like structure interior to the petals and exterior to the stamens in certain flowers and in milkweeds. Since most milkweeds have bent-back petals, the hoods typically are the most prominent feature of the flowers.

Hooded—arching over and partially concealing or shielding.

Horn—a small, round, or flattened projection from the hoods of milkweed flowers.

Host—as used in this guide, a plant from which a parasitic plant derives nourishment.

Hypanthium—a cup-shaped or tubular flower structure in which the sepals, petals, and stamens are fused together.

Inflorescence—an arrangement or cluster of flowers on an axis.

Infusion—a tealike beverage made by steeping plant parts (usually leaves) in hot water.

Involucre—a distinct series of bracts or leaves that enclose a flower or cluster of flowers; often used in descriptions of the Aster family (Asteraceae) flower heads.

Keel—a pair of united petals present in pea and other flowers.

Krummholz—term used to describe the stunted, windblown trees found at timberline. In German, *krumm* means "crooked," and *holz* means "wood."

Lance shaped or lanceolate—shaped like the head of a lance or spear; these leaves are significantly longer than wide, widest below the middle, and tapering toward the top.

Leaflet—a distinct, leaflike segment of a compound leaf.

Lobe—a segment of an incompletely divided plant part, typically rounded; often used in reference to leaves.

Margin—the edge of a leaf or petal.

Mat—densely interwoven or tangled low plant growth.

Nerve—a prominent vein in a leaf or organ.

Nodding—bending downward.

Node—point on a stem where one or more leaves or branches are attached.

Nut—a hard, dry fruit.

Nutlet—term for a small, hard, one-seeded fruit or segment of a fruit.

Oblong—often used to describe leaf shape; these leaves resemble a rectangle, but have rounded corners and are at least twice as long as wide.

Opposite—paired directly across from one another along a stem or axis; see **Alternate** (see illustration p. 9).

Ovary—the portion of the flower where the seeds develop, usually a swollen area below the style (if present) and stigma.

Ovate—egg shaped.

Palmate—spreading like the fingers of a hand (see illustration p. 9).

Palmately compound—leaf with three or more leaflets attached at the tip of the leaf stalk.

Panicle—an open or compact branching flower cluster with stalked flowers.

Parallel—side by side, approximately the same distance apart, for the entire length; often used in reference to veins or edges of leaves.

Perennial—a plant that lives for many years.

Petal—the component parts of the corolla, often the most brightly colored and visible parts of the flower.

Phyllaries—tiny modified leaves that cover the flower head in the Aster family (Asteraceae); also called bracts.

Pinnate—divided or lobed along each side of a leaf stalk, resembling a feather (see illustration p. 9).

Pistil—the seed-producing, or female, unit of a flower; consists of the ovary, style (if present), and stigma; a flower may have one to several separate pistils.

Pod—a dry fruit that splits open along the edges.

Pollen—tiny, often powdery, male reproductive cells formed in the stamens; typically necessary for seed production.

Poultice—a soft, sometimes heated dressing that is applied to the skin for medicinal purposes.

Prickle—a small, sharp, spinelike outgrowth from the outer surface.

Raceme—an unbranched stem with stalked flowers, the newest flowers forming at the top.

Ray flower—a flower in the Aster family (Asteraceae) with a single, strap-shaped corolla resembling one flower petal; ray flowers may surround the disk flowers in a flower head, or in some species such as dandelions, the flower heads may be composed entirely of ray flowers (see illustration p. 13).

Rhizome—an underground stem producing roots and shoots at the nodes.

Riparian—the corridor related to a river or stream.

Runner—a long, trailing stem.

Sap—the juice within a plant.

Sedge—a large group of grasslike plants, many of which grow in wetlands.

Sepal—a component part of the calyx, typically green but sometimes enlarged and brightly colored.

Serrate—possessing sharp, forward-pointing teeth.

Shrub—a small multistemmed, woody plant.

Simple Leaf—a leaf that has a single leaflike blade, although this may be lobed or divided (see illustration p. 9).

Species—the smallest unit of classification of living things; a group of very similar individuals that use their environment in a similar manner and are capable of mating with one another to produce viable offspring.

Specific epithet or name—the second portion of a scientific name, separating that species from all others. For instance, in *Aquilegia coerula* (Colorado columbine), *Aquilegia* is the genus, and *coerula* is the specific epithet or specific name.

Spike—an elongated, unbranched cluster of stalkless or nearly stalkless flowers.

Spine—a thin, stiff, sharply pointed projection.

Spreading—extending outward from; at right angles to; widely radiating.

Spur—a hollow tubular projection from the base of a petal or sepal; often produces nectar.

Stalk—as used in this guide, the stem supporting the leaf, flower, or flower cluster.

Stalkless—lacking a stalk; a stalkless leaf is attached directly to the stem at the leaf base.

Stamen—the male unit of a flower that produces the pollen; typically consisting of a long filament with a pollen-producing tip.

Staminodes—sterile stamens.

Standard—see **Banner**.

Sterile—in flowers, refers to an inability to produce seeds; in habitats, refers to poor nutrient and mineral availability in the soil.

Stigma—the portion of the pistil receptive to pollination; usually at the top of the style and often appearing fuzzy or sticky.

Stipule—a bract or leafy structure occurring in pairs at the base of the leaf stalk.

Style—the portion of the pistil between the ovary and the stigma; typically a slender stalk.

Subspecies—a group of plants within a species that has consistent, repeating, genetic, and structural distinctions; represented as "ssp." in scientific names.

Succulent—thickened and fleshy or juicy.

Taproot—a stout, main root extending downward.

Taxonomy—the ordering of plants and animals according to established criteria.

Tepals—petals and sepals that cannot be distinguished from each other.

Toothed—bearing teeth or sharply angled projections along the edge.

Tuber—a thick, creeping underground stem; sometimes also used to describe thickened portions of roots.

Tubercle—a small, rounded projection, as occurs on a cactus or a plant root.

Tubular—narrow, cylindrical, and tubelike.

Umbel—a flat-topped flower cluster in which each flower stalk grows from one point in a similar manner to the way the stays of an umbrella spread outward from the main umbrella stem; representative of the Parsley family (Apiaceae).

Variety—a group of plants within a species that has a distinct range, habitat, or structure. Represented as "var." in scientific names.

Veins—bundles of small tubes that carry water, minerals, and nutrients.

Whorl—three or more parts attached at the same point along a stem or axis and often surrounding the stem.

Winged—having thin bands of leaflike tissue attached edgewise along the length.

Wings—the two side petals flanking the keel in many flowers of the Bean family (Fabaceae).

Woody—firm-stemmed or branched.

WILDFLOWER RESOURCES

Allred, Kelly. *Flora Neomexicana II: Glossarium Nominum; A Lexicon of New Mexico Plant Names.* 2nd ed. Raleigh, NC: Lulu Enterprises, 2012.

Allred, Kelly, and Robert DeWitt Ivey. *Flora Neomexicana III: An Illustrated Identification Manual.* Raleigh, NC: Lulu Enterprises, 2012.

Anderson, Berta. *Wildflower Name Tales.* Colorado Springs, CO: Century One Press, 1976.

Carter, Jack L. *Trees and Shrubs of Colorado.* Boulder, CO: Johnson Books, 1988.

Coffey, Timothy. *The History and Folklore of North American Wildflowers.* Boston: Houghton Mifflin, 1994.

Colorado Native Plant Society. *Rare Plants of Colorado.* 2nd ed. Guilford, CT: FalconGuides, 1997.

Craighead, John J., Frank C. Craighead, and Ray J. Davis. *A Field Guide to Rocky Mountain Wildflowers: Northern Arizona and New Mexico to British Columbia.* Boston: Houghton Mifflin, 1987.

Cronquist, Alfred, et al. *Intermountain Flora.* 8 vols. Bronx, NY: New York Botanical Garden, 1972–2005.

Dahms, David. *Rocky Mountain Wildflowers Pocket Guide.* Windsor, CO: Paragon Press, 1999.

Duft, Joseph F., and Robert K. Mosely. *Alpine Wildflowers of the Rocky Mountains.* Missoula, MT: Mountain Press, 1989.

Elmore, Francis H. *Ethnobotany of the Navajo.* Albuquerque: University of New Mexico Press, 1972.

Guennel, C. K. *Guide to Colorado Wildflowers: Mountains.* Englewood, CO: Westcliffe Publishers, 1995.

Harrington, Harold D. *Manual of the Plants of Colorado.* Denver, CO: Sage Books, 1954.

Kershaw, Linda. *Edible & Medicinal Plants of the Rockies.* Edmonton, Canada: Lone Pine Publishing, 2000.

Kershaw, Linda, Andy MacKinnon, and Jim Pojar. *Plants of the Rocky Mountains.* Grand Rapids, MI: Lone Pine Publishing, 1998.

Moerman, Daniel E. *Medicinal Plants of Native America.* Ann Arbor: University of Michigan Museum of Anthropology, 1986.

Mutel, Cornelia F., and John C. Emerick. *From Grassland to Glacier.* Boulder, CO: Johnson Books, 1984.

Nelson, Ruth Ashton. *Handbook of Rocky Mountain Plants.* 4th ed. Revised by Roger L. Williams. Niwot, CO: Roberts Rinehart Publishers, 1992.

Pesman, M. W., *Meet the Natives: A Field Guide to Rocky Mountain Wildflowers, Trees, and Shrubs; Bridging the Gap between Trail and Garden.* 11th ed. Revised by David Johnson. Boulder, CO: Johnson Books, 2011.

Spellenberg, Richard. *Audubon Society Field Guide to North American Wildflowers, Western Region*. Rev. ed. New York: Alfred A. Knopf, 2001.

Weber, W. A., and R. C. Wittmann. *Colorado Flora: Eastern Slope*. 4th ed. Niwot: University Press of Colorado, 2012.

Weber, W. A., and R. C. Wittmann. *Colorado Flora: Western Slope*. 4th ed. Niwot: University Press of Colorado, 2012.

Willard, Beatrice E., and M. T. Smithson. *Alpine Wildflowers of the Rocky Mountains*. Estes Park, CO: Rocky Mountain Nature Association, 1988.

Wingate, Janet L., and L. Yeatts. *Alpine Flower Finder: The Key to Rocky Mountain Wildflowers Found Above Treeline*. Wingate Consulting, 2013.

Online and Electronic Resources

Biota of North America Program (BONAP)—Searchable, comprehensive, up-to-date database providing in-depth information on the taxonomy of the entire vascular flora of North America (excluding Mexico). http://bonap.org/

Colorado Rocky Mountain Wildflowers App—Developed by Al Schneider and Whitney Til for Apple and Android phones and tablets. Contains several thousand photos of 600 species from the foothills to the alpine zone. www.highcountryapps.com/

Eastern Colorado Wildflowers—A site with fantastic photos and bloom season information. www.easterncoloradowildflowers.com

Flora of North America—This vast 30-volume work in progress provides one comprehensive resource for information on the names, taxonomic relationships, continent-wide distributions, and morphological characteristics of all plants native and naturalized found in North America north of Mexico. http://floranorthamerica.org/; www.efloras.org

Native American Ethnobotany—A searchable database of plants used as drugs, foods, dyes, fibers, and more, by native peoples of North America. http://herb.umd.umich.edu/

Southwest Colorado Wildflowers—A comprehensive site covering the more common flowers seen in the Four Corners area. Full of great photos and extremely informative details about plants, their names, and the botanists who discovered them. www.swcoloradowildflowers.com

Synthesis of the Flora of North America, The—This DVD "database on the taxonomy, nomenclature, phytogeography, and biological attributes of [all] North American vascular flora" is the culmination of 40 years of work by John Kartesz. These DVDs provide over 150,000 photographs, plant descriptions, and county-by-county records of every plant in North America.

USDA Plants Database—This searchable database provides "standardized information about the vascular plants, mosses, liverworts, hornworts, and lichens of the U.S. and its territories." Includes synonyms, images, species information, and distribution maps. http://plants.usda.gov/java/

INDEX

ABOUT THE AUTHOR

Chris Kassar is a conservation biologist, guide, and writer with a reverence for nature, a thirst for adventure, and a desire to leave the world a little bit better. She gained extensive knowledge about wildflowers and plants through various field courses, formal studies in pursuit of her master's degree in wildlife biology at Utah State, and her work as a biologist, guide, environmental educator, and interpreter in various national forests and parks across the West, including Rocky Mountain, Denali, Arches, and Canyonlands.

Over the past few years, Chris has also turned her attention to using words and imagery to document various adventures, bring attention to important issues, and advocate for environmental change. She runs Rios Libres, an environmental nonprofit dedicated to protecting rivers in Chile from dams, and she also works as senior editor of *Elevation Outdoors Magazine.* Chris is also a freelance writer and photographer with published works in numerous publications, including *Climbing, Mother Jones,* the *Boston Globe Magazine, National Geographic Adventure,* and *Women's Adventure Magazine.* Chris, who is most at peace in the outdoors and considers a successful year one in which she spends more nights sleeping under the stars than under a ceiling, lives in Salida, Colorado. Learn more at www.chriskassar.com.

THE ROCKY MOUNTAIN CONSERVANCY

The Rocky Mountain Conservancy promotes stewardship of Rocky Mountain National Park and similar lands through education and philanthropy.